Living Well with A Lor Health Condition

Living well with a long-term health condition is one of the most challenging experiences one can have. Written based on the most recent research evidence, this straightforward guide to managing both the emotional and physical aspects of chronic illness gives practical suggestions of how those living with a range of conditions can most effectively manage their symptoms whilst still living an active and fulfilling life.

Covering a range of topics including self-management of pain, fatigue, stress and lifestyle changes, and adapting to a diagnosis, the book provides an accessible resource that will enable patients and carers to better understand and meet the psychological challenges of a long-term condition. By taking a holistic approach, Bogosian empowers the individual to identify their own goals and the pathways to achieve them to reach personal satisfaction, while negotiating the complexities of their condition.

This book will be an indispensable guide to those living with a long-term illness, as well as their family members. It will also be of interest to specialist nurses, care consultants, or social workers working with people with a chronic illness.

Angeliki Bogosian is a health psychologist and academic working at City, University of London, UK.

Living Well with A Long-Term Health Condition

An Evidence-Based Guide to Managing Your Symptoms

Angeliki Bogosian

Routledge
Taylor & Francis Group

LONDON AND NEW YORK

First published 2020
by Routledge
2 Park Square, Milton Park, Abingdon, Oxon OX14 4RN

and by Routledge
52 Vanderbilt Avenue, New York, NY 10017

Routledge is an imprint of the Taylor & Francis Group, an informa business

© 2020 Angeliki Bogosian

The right of Angeliki Bogosian to be identified as author of this work has been asserted by her in accordance with sections 77 and 78 of the Copyright, Designs and Patents Act 1988.

Trademark notice: Product or corporate names may be trademarks or registered trademarks, and are used only for identification and explanation without intent to infringe.

British Library Cataloguing-in-Publication Data
A catalogue record for this book is available from the British Library

Library of Congress Cataloging-in-Publication Data
A catalog record for this book has been requested

ISBN: 978-1-138-21112-4 (hbk)
ISBN: 978-1-138-21113-1 (pbk)
ISBN: 978-1-315-45357-6 (ebk)

Typeset in Sabon
by Apex CoVantage, LLC

Contents

Preface

'Living well' may sound like a lofty, if somewhat abstract goal, but it is something that we can all define and attain. Some planning and discipline are required, but it can be done. First, we need to identify our definition of living well. What activities in our day give us pleasure and a sense of achievement? Then we find how to modify things to get those things done. We have to learn how to be in the world and how to engage in meaningful pursuits within our limits. This book explores ways to live well with a long-term condition.

As a health psychologist, I examine how people adjust to long-term conditions, developing and delivering psychological programmes to help people adapt to their circumstances. For my master's degree dissertation, I interviewed partners of people newly diagnosed with multiple sclerosis. For my PhD thesis, I conducted a series of studies with children who have a parent with multiple sclerosis, which included interviews with children and parents. Later on, I facilitated mindfulness groups with people with multiple sclerosis and Parkinson's disease. I have also worked in research projects and supervised doctoral theses that examined how people adjust in other chronic conditions, like diabetes, asthma, chronic pulmonary disease and functional neurological disorder.

Through the research interviews I conducted or supervised, I learned a lot from people's stories. I discovered how they manage their condition, what they found helpful or unhelpful. The patients' groups I facilitate are based on mindfulness principals, and they are specifically tailored to the needs of people who are dealing with conditions that progress over time. Again, through these groups I've learned a lot about what actually works and what doesn't work and how people use the techniques they learn in various aspects of their lives.

The stories presented here are not based on real people; they are a realistic amalgamation of different interviews and discussions with people with a long-term condition as well as discussions with colleagues and their experiences working with people with long-term conditions.

Apart from scientific articles and handbooks, I also love reading popular psychology books. Books about relationships, productivity, overcoming difficulties, personal development; you name it, I have read it. Some of the books I've read changed my life and my perspective. However, I don't like books that are too prescriptive. Initially, it's comforting to be given specific guidelines but following someone else's path requires a lot of effort, which is no way to live with ease and authenticity. The books that I find particularly helpful are the books that present ideas through stories about people – people who are faced with dilemmas and make choices. This was the kind of book I wanted to write. Writing down everything I learned over the years working in the field in a consistent, organised way helped me refine my understanding. Now it is time to release this knowledge into the world in the hopes you will find it useful in your journey to living well with a long-term health condition. Maybe this book will offer some ideas of how our thoughts, emotions and bodies are connected. Perhaps the stories described here will inspire you to change something in your life. Maybe they will nudge you to experiment with some new ways of being or doing.

Having a long-term condition is one of the many things you have going in your life. You need to manage the symptoms of the condition, but also you want time to enjoy your life. A key message of the book is that you do not need to spend all of your time and energy attending to the health condition. Of course, there will be times when you need to focus almost solely on the long-term condition, for example, to take care of an exacerbation. But when things are settled, you can use the rest of your time and energy to create a life you love, where you follow your dreams, listen to your needs and connect with people you love. Reflect on how you manage your condition at the moment and how much space the condition takes up in your life, let go of things that do not serve you anymore and add more of the things that make your life fuller. No matter the limits, you can find ways to either continue with activities you always enjoyed or find suitable alternatives.

Introduction

Joe

Joe had a good day after all. He woke up with stiffness and pain in his left leg, which made getting out of bed and preparing breakfast a long and arduous process. But he was excited to see Albert, who helps him with his garden. Joe could no longer kneel, dig or pull, so he asked Albert to come around and help him once a fortnight. Albert isn't much of a gardener but diligently follows Joe's instructions. For Joe, his garden is his great love and joy. He has a clear and precise plan of how he wants his yard to look and knows how to care for his plants.

After nearly four hours of work, Albert left, and Joe had a light snack and a cup of tea on his sun-drenched patio. He loved looking at his garden. Waking up every day to his growing plants gave him immense joy. When his condition progressed, and he could not work in the yard anymore, he felt devastated. But after a few months of feeling low, he met Albert, a journalism student lodging at his neighbour's semi-detached house. He hadn't thought of asking others to help him with his garden before, but things needed to change now. He used to enjoy the feeling of earth between his fingers. But there were other aspects to gardening that he could still enjoy, like experimenting with different plant varieties and looking out at his garden.

Much has been written about leading a good life and adapting to circumstances. I was always drawn to stories of people who, despite imposed physical, mental or cultural limits, lead a happy life, a life full of challenges and achievements. Interviewing and working with people with long-term conditions and their partners in my professional life as a psychologist and a researcher has taught me a lot. The most remarkable point I have learned is how adaptable human beings can be, and that physical limits do not necessarily mean lower quality of life. When I use the term long-term condition in this book, I mean a physical health issue that cannot be cured but can be kept under control through medical treatment and personal efforts. A vast number of conditions are considered long-term and include stroke, diabetes, renal disease, cancer, Alzheimer's, Parkinson's, multiple sclerosis, bronchitis, asthma, hypertension, irritable bowel syndrome, chronic back pain, chronic respiratory syndrome, bipolar disorder, migraine; the list is long. Of course, these conditions come with different sets of issues to manage, from adhering to a complicated medical regime to managing stress, work and personal relationships.

Learning to live well with a long-term condition has become more critical than ever. The philosopher, Ivan Illich in his book *Medical Nemesis* argued: "the greatest future achievement in medicine will not be some new technological achievement, but if we can better support people to look after themselves".[1] More than 15 million people in the UK live with a long-term medical disease that cannot currently be cured, and recent evidence suggests that the number is set to rise by 23% over the next 25 years.[2]

When faced with a long-term condition an individual faces many issues. These may include maintaining a healthy lifestyle, sound sleep habits, managing stress, making decisions about when to seek medical help and what treatments to try, working effectively with your health care team, using medications safely and efficiently, finding and using community resources, talking about your illness with family and friends and adapting social activities. The discipline of health psychology that I will be drawing from in this book is very much built around changing health behaviours and navigating through the tasks needed to manage a long-term condition.

Unravelling all the difficulties involved can be extremely valuable. Looking at the context and the severity of each one and how it links with other challenges can give us a clearer picture of what is going on and how to deal with it. In **Chapter 1**, you will create a list of things you want to change or cope with, then prioritise the items. Which challenge do you want to address first and which problem can stay unresolved for the time being? Identifying and carefully prioritising your needs is the vital first step.

When newly diagnosed with a condition, a lot of questions and worries are swirling around your mind: how can I make this work? How can I achieve the things I want to if I am in pain? How can I accomplish anything if I feel fatigued the minute I wake up? Will I be able to hold on to my job? And so on. Things have changed or might change in the future. Uncertainty about prognosis can make planning and adapting to your condition even more challenging. So, how do you sustain a happy life despite these difficulties?

Emotional difficulties emerge when what we do differs from our goals and self-standards.[3] For example, if your goal is to get a promotion in a very competitive industry and due to increased fatigue you cannot always deliver high-quality projects in a short period, there will be a significant discrepancy between your performance and your goal. Therefore, the first task is to examine what has changed and what you want to change in order to set appropriate action plans and relevant goals.

In **Chapter 2**, you will create a list of the goals and activities that make your life full and meaningful. It is not always necessary to have specific goals; some things are worth doing just for the sheer pleasure of doing them. We nourish our soul when we lose ourselves to pastimes, without always aiming to accomplish anything in particular. Winston Churchill liked to paint, Woody Allen plays the saxophone and Steve Jobs loved calligraphy. If you can't think of 'just for fun' activities, think of things you used to enjoy when you were a child. I liked making 'magazines' when I was a kid, making collages and writing up little stories. Now, my creative outlet is making journals and decorating notebooks simply for my pleasure. The key is that all these activities align with your personal values.

Jane

Jane was diagnosed with relapsing-remitting multiple sclerosis and worked as a legal secretary in a very busy firm. Jane was the office factotum. In the evenings, she looked after her 3-year-old twin daughters. She was always striving to achieve the best in all her roles. Jane was very organised and proactive and still on top of things. During her relapses, she had an especially hard time keeping up with all the demands. Her fatigue was so severe that she could hardly move her body. She knew that she needed to reduce her hours but was reluctant to do so because it would have felt like giving in to her condition. However, she was unhappy and permanently tired.

There was a turning point just before the Christmas holidays. She was working 12-hour shifts in her firm for three consecutive days. And one afternoon everything went blurry. She remembers her colleagues asking her if she felt OK, then she remembers lying on a sofa in the waiting room in her firm. How she got to the hospital and what happened there is blurred but what is clear is her neurologist telling her he would sign her off work and she needed to consider giving up her job. This was a massive shock for Jane. When she discussed the neurologist's advice with her family, they urged her to quit and told her how worried they had been with her long hours. That was surprising; she thought she could still do everything as before she was diagnosed. She was torn.

After lengthy discussions with her husband and her friends and weighing the pros and cons she decided to reduce her hours for a while but eventually, she gave up work. She now works with a charity, and her role involves organising theatre outings for people with disabilities. She loves the theatre and loves feeling useful, and this was the best combination of her passions. She missed working with others and socialising after work, so her work with the charity provided a good social outlet. And even though her goals were now very different to the ones she once had, her goals still made her happy since they fulfilled her need to be useful and to interact with others on a day-to-day basis.

Once you have a list of goals and activities you would like to pursue, you can go through the items and think: can I still achieve all those things? If yes, great! Make sure each day you spend some of your time working on those activities. If not, no problem. You have options. One option is to focus on one or two critical areas of the goal.[4] Another option is to shift your focus entirely from long-term goals to shorter-term goals, even daily goals. Finally, a third option is to adapt these goals in a way that allows you to still achieve them.[5] For example, if one of the activities you'd like to pursue is writing a memoir about your journey with a long-term condition, but you do not feel you could achieve this, you could focus on just one or two key areas like searching and learning about the condition. You could also keep a log of symptoms and jot down a couple of thoughts about them. There is also the possibility of focusing on shorter goals; for example, write blog posts about your experience with the long-term condition. A third option would be to adapt the goal – could you for example ask other people with long-term conditions to co-write the book with you? Like Joe did – he could not enjoy all aspects of gardening, but he held on to some aspects (e.g. planning what to plant and where) and delegated others (e.g. digging).

Sometimes, we hang on to our set goals for too long. It is disheartening not to be able to achieve specific goals or to have to let go of treasured goals. We may not be able to think clearly of other alternatives, and we end up investing too much time and energy on something that does not serve us anymore. Long-term condition or not, we all change over time. Things that used to be important before may not necessarily be important anymore. From time to time we need to review whether what we strive for is what we truly want. It is also difficult to know when letting go is resignation and when it is the right choice. But as with all things, it does get more comfortable with practice. The more you evaluate your goals against your current circumstances and dreams, the more you sharpen your ability to know when you need to push a little harder, when to adjust and when to let go.

When you are diagnosed with a long-term condition, you do not necessarily feel 'ill' or at least you don't feel ill all the time. You feel like you, with some symptoms or limitations that you need to accept or learn to manage. Your personal temperament, your age, your past experiences, your psychological state when you received the diagnosis, the symptoms of the illness, social support and financial resources will all influence the impact of the condition on your life. Unfortunately, we cannot control many of these factors. In this book, I will focus on the factors that we can control and discuss what to do about the ones we cannot control.

Of course, the best possible scenario is to cure these long-term conditions once and for all. To stop the pain, get rid of the fatigue, start walking again and not have to inject yourself ever again. Researchers in all fields are working hard to find cures and a lot of money has been invested towards that goal. But while we are waiting for all these to happen, we can find ways to manage the symptoms and their effects better, to minimise their impact on our lives so they do not take over our lives.

Having some tools to get more control over thoughts, emotions and physical symptoms is my goal in writing this book. When we have some difficulty in certain areas of our lives, an overwhelming feeling can infuse all other areas. We generalise, we feel like everything is wrong, and nothing can be done. It is OK, we all do this.

In **Chapter 3**, we will look at how you can best manage stress, to reduce its physical and psychological impact. Having a long-term condition may push you to re-define the limits of your body. The chapters that follow will describe how one gets on with life after the diagnosis and, if your condition changes, how to adapt to the shifting landscape. What I will be discussing in this book is based on scientific evidence that shows what works and what doesn't for a lot of individuals. A lot of the advice is also based on health psychology theories that provide some explanation of why things are the way they are and how things often pan out. Of course, you are the expert of your condition and you can decide what may work for you and discard the rest.

The stories presented in this book can show you a different perspective. They will not tell you what and what not to do, but they will show you a road map with different paths and turns, traps and resting spots. Experiment with picturing yourself in different scenarios, test different ways of thinking and make those stories the examples to avoid or follow. The stories may provide insight into something you are going through now or may do in the future. You might not always agree with the advice, and that is fine. You make the rules. Tailor things to your unique circumstances. This book is by no means a cookbook; life is not simple as that. Think through the ideas presented here, discuss them with others and debate the pros and cons before you reach your conclusions.

There is a vast number of health conditions and I will not cover them all here. What I will do is discuss some common symptoms that a lot of people with different long-term conditions experience: pain, fatigue and sleep difficulties (**Chapter 4**). I will also cover ways to cultivate some psychological skills that could help you along the way, like having more control over your thoughts, adopting a positive frame of mind, developing self-compassion and building up your uncertainty tolerance (**Chapter 5**).

Making lifestyle changes, as will be discussed in **Chapter 6**, can help you towards a healthy body and mind, which will be useful especially when coping with troublesome symptoms. Learning ways to help you adhere to your medical regime, exercise more and make healthier food choices will move you towards a healthier body. Further, learning more about how motivation works, how to believe in your skills and how to form new habits and change old ones can support you in your journey to a healthier lifestyle, make you more resilient and help you keep going when things are getting tough.

A common thread throughout the book is that you are the best person to know what is going on in your body and the only person who is in charge and can change things. That's not to say that you have to do everything on your own. In fact, in **Chapter 7** I will discuss how relationships can help you emotionally and practically. I will offer some tips on how you can deepen your relationships with others and how to improve your communication. Of course, managing relationships with health care professionals, partners and children could not have been excluded from this chapter, as well as some tips if you are living on your own and you want to boost your social circle.

The final chapter (**Chapter 8**) will bring together everything discussed earlier in the book and suggest ways to put things that make sense to you into practice to design your own life. Customise everything written in this book against your dimensions, be an active participant in this book. See whether some adjustments need to be made to fit your circumstances, maybe see whether specific tips might work better for you when used for a different issue. To make psychological advice useful, we need to be open and curious, and we also need a critical mind. Test things out, set out small experiments to see whether and how something works. Maybe start by setting up a little test and later on use a technique with something that is more troublesome or harder to control. You will not have to do every single thing in this book. This is meant as a toolkit with different techniques that you can choose depending on the symptoms and issues you experience, and you might want to come back to individual chapters if you need to pick up something else later on. People with long-term conditions usually say they have good days and bad days. This book is, at least in part, about trying to have more of the good days that make up the mosaic of our lives.

Chapter overview

Chapter 1: Discusses how to identify things that have changed and things you might change as well as some ideas on how to respond to frustrations related to your condition. The chapter also includes some exercises on how to prioritise challenges you would like to focus on.

Chapter 2: The focus of the chapter is on the 'why' you want to make changes. If you want to make changes, what motivates you to make those changes? The aim is to help you refine your aims in life that will direct your efforts to a happier and more meaningful life.

Chapter 3: This chapter addresses how the mind and body are connected and can influence one another; also how to manage stress.

Chapter 4: Here, I will discuss how to manage common physical symptoms: pain, fatigue and sleep difficulties.

Chapter 5: Cultivating some psychological and behavioural skills could help you not only with the management of specific symptoms but also with the smoother control of other areas in your life. Specifically, the chapter will present some ways to deal with negative thoughts using mindfulness principles, adopt a positive frame of mind, become more compassionate and increase your uncertainty tolerance.

Chapter 6: Suggestions on how to form and maintain healthy habits will be discussed. These healthy habits include adherence to medication, diet changes, exercise and quitting smoking.

Chapter 7: Here, I will discuss how relationships can help you emotionally and practically. Relationships can also indirectly help boost your immunity and health. I will offer some tips on how you can deepen your relationships with others (health care professionals, partners, children) and how to improve your communication and expand your social circle.

Chapter 8: This chapter will bring together everything discussed in the book and suggest ways to put the ideas in practice to design your own life.

Bibliography

1 Illich I. *Medical Nemesis the Exploration of Health*. Random House; 1988.

2 *Long Term Conditions Compendium of Information Third Edition*.; 2012. www.dh.gov.uk/publications. Accessed March 8, 2019.

3 Carver CS, Lawrence JW, Scheier MF. Self-Discrepancies and Affect: Incorporating the Role of Feared Selves. *Personality and Social Psychology Bulletin*. 1999;25(7):783–792. doi:10.1177/0146167299025007002

4 Carver CS, Sutton SK, Scheier MF. Action, Emotion, and Personality: Emerging Conceptual Integration. *Personality and Social Psychology Bulletin*. 2000;26(6):741–751. doi:10.1177/0146167200268008

5 Bogosian A, Morgan M, Bishop FL, Day F, Moss-Morris R. Adjustment Modes in the Trajectory of Progressive Multiple Sclerosis: A Qualitative Study and Conceptual Model. *Psychology and Health*. 2017;32(3). doi:10.1080/08870446.2016.1268691

Chapter 1

Itinerary
What has changed or needs to change

The body is beautifully made. It just works. It does its thing, and we get on with life. We create art, we bring up children, pursue a career, travel, bond with people, cultivate interests and hobbies. But the time comes when something is not working well. Symptoms prevent us from doing what we want to do. And then what? When the body changes, do we change? Can we still be us, when we can no longer do the things we used to do?

Yes, we can. We are more than the sum of the symptoms we experience. The core of us remains unchanged, despite the changes in the weather around us. No one wants to be ill, and no one wants to experience painful and ability-limiting symptoms, but the reality is that most of us will at some point in our life. For the most part, it is beyond our control whether and what kind of long-term condition we will get. What we can control is how much the illness influences our lives.

The first step to taking back some control is to understand the condition. This means learning about what causes the illness, its symptoms, what medical treatments are available and what you can you do to manage the symptoms. It also means observing how the condition and its treatment affects you. Most long-term conditions go up and down in intensity and don't follow a steady path. It is useful to know your path, the symptoms their intensity and their patterns, what exacerbates them and what alleviates them.

With a long-term condition, you become more aware of your body. Minor symptoms previously ignored may now cause concerns. For example, is my chest pain a sign of a heart attack? Is this pain in my knee a sign that the arthritis is getting worse? And things get more complicated if you experience more than one long-term condition. According to NHS England,[1] of the people who report they live with long-term conditions, 24% have two long-term conditions and 20% live with three or more long-term conditions. In the case of multiple long-term conditions, it is even harder to determine which symptoms can be assigned to which condition. There are no simple, reassuring answers. Nor is there a fail-safe way of sorting out serious signals from minor temporary symptoms that can be ignored. It is helpful to know and understand the natural rhythm of your condition(s). In general, if your symptoms are unusual, severe, persistent or occur after starting a new medication or changes in the dose of your medication they should be checked out with your doctor.[2]

Taking it all in

Blanche

Blanche is known for her perfectionism and discipline. She is a floor manager at one of the biggest luxury goods shops in London, responsible for seven members of staff and for the recent 20% increase in sales in her department. It was Christmas, the busiest period of the year, when some strange issues appeared. Once working tirelessly, 12-hours a day, now Blanche felt tired and achy from the minute she woke up. Arriving home, all she wanted to do was lie in bed. The fatigue and the pain increased over time, causing anxiety, perplexity, fear – and sometimes, guilt. For Blanche was always a reliable worker, always on top of things and now she was distracted and forgetful and too tired after work to spend time with her husband and two young daughters, three and five years old. Blanche did not want to disappoint her employers, especially during the Christmas period, so she pushed through. Every single day was a struggle, but every single day she was there, at the shop. Finally, Christmas day arrived, and she spent all day in bed, unable to do as much as sit up to eat some of the Christmas dinner her husband had prepared. Well aware that a combination of the flu and work stress could have played havoc with her body, Blanche decided to take a week off work to rest. The week that followed was one of the strangest in her life. She could not move her body. Blanche felt like she was trapped in a jelly-like world, and every move required ten times the effort. A week passed, two weeks passed, and things did not improve. Blanche thought it was time to see her doctor, who took a careful medical history, took her blood pressure and some blood samples. The blood pressure was good, and the blood samples did not show anaemia, under-active thyroid or any liver or kidney problems, yet the lymph nodes in her neck were enlarged, indicating an infection. Unable to diagnose anything, her doctor sent her home with the instruction to rest for two more weeks hoping the symptoms will clear up. Unfortunately, things did not improve, but nevertheless, Blanche tried to get back to work, albeit, with not much success. The days she managed to get in the store, she could not think clearly and felt she was more of a hindrance than a help. Her doctor signed her off work for two months, which was then extended to four months and finally to six months. Blanche was devastated. It was so difficult for her not to work. She liked to give advice to less-experienced staff members, she loved the buzz of the shop floor, but she could not cope anymore with the stress of her work or the long hours.

After a few months and numerous medical tests, she was told that she had Myalgic Encephalitis, also known as Chronic Fatigue Syndrome. The causes and timeline of the condition are unclear. Her doctor suggested reserving her energy, getting into a regular but gentle exercise routine, a balanced diet and recommended going to a 6-week stress-management course.

For the best part of a year, Blanche was hindered by her condition, confused and worried about what was going on. But over time her condition became a smaller feature in her life. Once she had a name for her condition, she was able to make peace with the fact that this was something that she would need to deal with in the long run. She decided "It's best to outsmart your condition, rather than battle it head on". Leaving emotions aside, she tried to solve each medical issue methodically, the way she approached work issues, examining what was wrong and brainstorming how best to solve them. Blanche was able to let go of wanting things to be different, of wanting her condition to be cured, and she started to live her life.

Preceding lengthy periods of medical tests, hospital appointments and uncertainty, the diagnosis comes with mixed emotions. Finding out about your condition can be upsetting, but also it can be a relief. When diagnosed you might have felt devastated, overwhelmed or completely numb. There are no right or wrong ways to feel. Emotions have a 'mind' of their own; they come up without an invitation.

Feeling anxious is very common and usual in the early stages of the condition and after significant changes. When living with a long-term condition, it might be difficult at times to keep a positive attitude, especially when you feel unwell and your future appears uncertain. As a result, you may feel frustrated, angry, demoralised, worried, anxious or depressed at times. Feeling low and at a loss is normal and to be expected. Although small levels of distress can push us into action and motivate changes, being significantly depressed or anxious might have an adverse impact on the prognosis of the condition or even worsen the symptoms.

There are two ways that the emotional response can affect the condition: via behaviour or via the physiological changes that emotions create. Feeling tense, angry, embarrassed, stressed, anxious or low in mood produces physiological changes such as increased tremor and muscle pain, impaired memory and concentration, and poor sleep. Even if we try to shut out these emotions or ignore them, we usually still suffer the physiological effects. There are also some indications that depression is linked to alterations in the immune system,[3] including for example in MS, researchers found depression was linked with increases in proinflammatory cytokine activity and inflammation.[4] Research has shown that chronic depression is associated with clinical and immunological progression of HIV/AIDS, i.e. decline in CD4+ T cells.[5] However, it is still unclear whether the depression caused the changes in the immune response or whether the immune response changes caused either depressive symptoms or progression of the condition which then led to depression. Furthermore, low mood and feeling numb may rob us of the motivation to make necessary lifestyle changes, such as changing eating habits, quitting smoking, exercising or taking medications as prescribed. Consequently, these behaviours can exacerbate the condition. For example, 18% of people living with a long-term condition smoke[1] and the people who smoke are more likely to have flare-ups in their condition and therefore more likely to be admitted to hospital.

Separating symptoms from their emotional impact

To discuss how best to manage your symptoms, we need to talk about the specific and most common challenges that people face. We know the answer to this question in rich detail thanks to many studies where researchers collected data on the most common problems through questionnaires or interviews. The illness demands can be broadly categorised in three-ways:

- *illness related*: learning to manage illness-related symptoms, such as pain, fatigue, complex treatment regimes and drugs side effects as well as learning to deal with a range of health care staff, hospital environments and treatments
- *emotional demands*: such as preserving emotional balance, self-image and sense of mastery and control, and preparing for an uncertain future
- *social demands*: continuing your social life, sustaining existing relationships and leisure activities.

It is not uncommon to be faced with a combination of physiological and emotional symptoms. With long-term conditions, many people assume that their symptoms are due solely to the disease itself. Although the disease can cause pain, shortness of breath, fatigue and the like, it is not the only cause. Each of the symptoms can contribute to the other symptoms, and all these can feed on each other. For example, depression causes fatigue, pain causes physical limitations, and these can lead to poor sleep and more fatigue. The interactions can then make the condition worse and create a vicious cycle that will get worse unless we find a way to break it. Besides, for some conditions these challenges will remain stable, for others, they will progress, or the symptoms will come and go at irregular intervals. When discussing later on in the book how best to manage symptoms, we will also consider the stable, progressive or cyclical nature of the symptoms.

Symptoms different timelines

Timeline	Description	Examples
Stable	The symptom appears and does not change over time; does not improve or worsen	Loss of motor function in traumatic brain injury
Progressive	The symptom appears and overtime, it gets worse. The deterioration can be fast or slow.	Motor challenges in Parkinson's disease
Cyclical	The symptom appears, but then it will entirely or partly improve	Relapses in multiple sclerosis

The symptoms and combinations of symptoms will also interact with other factors, like the illness prognosis, the available medical treatments, the severity of the symptoms, the interference of the symptoms in everyday life and also the stage of your life and other personal, financial or family circumstances. These other factors will have an impact on the way you feel, think and act. And consequently, the way you feel, think and act will have an effect on your symptoms.

Unfortunately, we cannot control a lot of these factors, things like the stage of your life when you get the illness, the illness prognosis or the symptoms of the condition. However, what we can control is the way we respond to those symptoms. We can control the way we relate to our thoughts and feelings and the choices we make. Even though sometimes it feels like you have no power over the long-term condition, you do have control over how much you let your condition influence your life.

Suppose you have problems getting to sleep. If you are frustrated or worried about the consequences of your lack of sleep, you could end up with anxiety about your insomnia and the more anxious you are, the less you sleep. These secondary emotions are unpleasant, unhelpful and a drain on our energy and vitality. And then you may get angry, anxious or depressed about that. This leads to a vicious cycle (see Figure 1.1). To break the vicious cycle, do

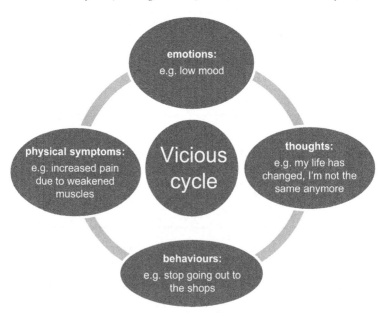

Figure 1.1 Vicious cycle of symptoms

something counterintuitive: whatever emotion shows up, no matter how unpleasant, don't struggle with it: notice it and let it go. Thus, when anxiety shows up, it's not a problem. Sure, it's unpleasant, and you don't like it, but it's nothing terrible. Sometimes your anxiety will be high, sometimes low, and sometimes there will be no anxiety at all. But more importantly, we do not waste our time and energy struggling with it.

I am not listing all the challenges and the complexity of it all to make you feel uncomfortable. The realisation of what has changed is the first step to prepare for the challenges to come.

But what if we approach the condition with its symptoms differently? What if we started with a blank slate? What if we view each symptom as a problem that needs solving, as Blanche did, as a challenge that is not personal?

A good way to avoid having your symptoms ruling your life is to approach them in a detached way. Do not over-identify with them; when you are describing them to someone else or to yourself, stick to the description of the physical sensations and try to explain them without emotion. Approach your symptoms and challenges almost from an administrative point of view. Think like a manager that faces logistic challenges and has to find a way around them. Your symptoms are not who you are and don't need to control your actions, they are issues that you could find a way around.

It's a delicate balance attending to your symptoms and at the same time not over-identifying with them. This does not mean that you don't feel upset or angry or that you ignore your emotions. But you can separate the emotions from the symptoms and do what you need to do despite having negative emotions towards your symptoms. The symptoms are what they are, you cannot get rid of them altogether, but you can find ways to make them interfere less with what is important to you. By approaching the symptoms in this way, we are able to see them more clearly and judge their interference. Then we have better quality information on what is going on. We can either relate this back to a doctor or come up with creative solutions to minimise the interference of the symptoms.

Leave aside, for a while, the impact and complications of the condition. Just think about the different aspects of the condition that need care.

If you haven't thought about the specifics of your condition, I encourage you to spend a few minutes mulling it over. You can even create a list of the symptoms of the condition and the changes it has created. Knowing the condition is the first step to guide your action plan of what needs to be done – if anything. It is impossible to tackle all aspects of the condition all in one go. First, we look at what is happening; then we deal with the rest. Some of those tasks will be easy to tackle and some of them more difficult and even impossible, but rather than considering them all together as a big impossible task, let's look at them as separate issues, without qualifying them as straightforward or taxing, without judging them as awful or insufferable. They are what they are. Having the tasks and issues laid out like this will help you see them more clearly. You can make decisions on how to tackle each, while at the same time, they won't take up too much space in your mind or weigh you down emotionally and you can direct some of this energy to the task that is truly important to you, no matter how small or big.

You don't let your condition weigh you down, so you save yourself a lot of time and energy. Of course, there will be times that a relapse, an exacerbation or progression of the condition, will mean that your focus needs to change and be placed on dealing with the condition. That's part of the process, part of the cycle, and you need to be alert enough and flexible enough to change gears when it is required. But eventually, things will settle, and you will find your new balance between managing your condition and leading a full life.

Oliver Sacks, the neurologist, widely known for his work on best sellers like, *Awakenings*, *The man who mistook his wife for a hat* and others, drew on his patients and his own experiences of dealing with long-term conditions in his work. He believed that illness need not rob us of our essential selves – and this was something he exemplified in his final months, as he continued to write remarkable essays even as cancer began to sap his strength and overwhelm him. Sacks understood our ability to adapt and emphasised that the capacity for someone to adjust to a particular condition – amnesia, blindness, deafness, migraines, phantom-limb syndrome, Asperger's syndrome and countless other conditions – cannot be known from the outset.

A lot of people see their condition as a journey to wellness and keep blogs, write books and share their stories. A notable example is Toni Bernhard, with her blog *Turning Straw into Gold*, who has authored three books related to her journey and discoveries and many more blogs and books chronicling the journey to find a balance and live life to the fullest. Researchers from the University of Melbourne collected all the evidence about the effects of social media use in long-term illness and found that social media can have a positive effect when it comes to gaining support and information.[6] You might find it useful to read about other people's stories and even keep your account of what is helping or not or identifying patterns with your health, e.g. when the pain feels better or worse.

Another way to keep a record of your self-management journey while at the same time process your thoughts and emotions is by using the expressive writing technique. Research has shown some positive effects of expressive writing on our physical and emotional health.

Expressive writing is when your writing pays more attention to feelings than the events or the people involved in the narrative. Your entries might look like stories with a beginning, middle and end but more often than not, expressive writing is messy and unpredictable. The connection between expressive writing and well-being was studied by Prof. James Pennebaker, at the University of Texas, Austin.[7] In his seminal research project, Pennebaker developed an expressive writing prompt to uncover the potential health benefits of writing about emotional upheaval. He asked students to spend 15 minutes writing about the most significant trauma of their lives or if they hadn't experienced a trauma, their most challenging time.

They were told to include their most profound thoughts, even if they had never shared these thoughts before. The students wrote in this way for four consecutive days. Then he monitored how often the students have visited the health centre and compared them with a group of students who spent the same amount of writing about something neutral, like their dorm room. The study showed that the students who were writing about their feelings had significantly less doctor appointments in the subsequent months[8] than the students who were writing about neutral topics.

These research findings have been replicated in subsequent research with people with long-term condition like asthma, arthritis, breast cancer and migraines. For example, in a small study conducted in Kansas,[9] it was found that women with breast cancer experienced fewer symptoms and had fewer cancer-related appointments in the months after doing expressive writing. Looking across all studies that have been conducted on the potential benefits of expressive writing for women with breast cancer, it was found that women who were on the expressive writing interventions reported less physical symptoms compared to the ones in the control group.[10] Of course, these results do not suggest that expressive writing will affect the cancer prognosis, and that was not the intention of the researchers either. But the results suggest that in the short term women who wrote about their feelings around cancer seemed to have better health when compared to women who wrote about facts of cancer.

Expressive writing is not a panacea and in fact, researchers led by Joanne Fratarolli[11] from the University of California Riverside pulled together 146 studies on expressive writing that showed a positive but small overall effect. With findings in the wound healing research area showing the most consistent positive outcomes. In the wound healing studies, brave volunteers typically do some expressive writing, and a few days later, after they are given a local anaesthetic, researchers removed a punch-size skin from their inner arm. The wound is typically 4 mm across and heals within 14 days. The healing of the wound is monitored, and it happens faster if people have spent time beforehand writing down their emotional personal thoughts.

Interestingly, expressive writing does not only work before you are wounded but can also work if you do it after. This means we can use expressive writing not only when surgery is planned, but also when unpredictable[12] injuries happen in everyday life.[9]

But how can writing about your emotions help? Initially, it was assumed that people felt better because they expressed previously bottled-up emotions. But then Pennebaker began looking more closely at the language people used in their writing.[13]

He found that people whose wounds healed the fastest changed the words they used as they kept writing. Whereas they started by using the word 'I' a lot, in later essays they moved on to saying 'he' or 'she' more often, suggesting they were looking at the event from other perspectives. They also used words like 'because', implying they were making sense of the events and putting them into a narrative.

Another explanation might be that through writing people found a way of managing their emotions. This explanation is supported by evidence showing that imagining a traumatic event and then writing a story about it also makes wounds heal faster.

After the first day of writing, most people say that churning up the past has made them feel worse. Does the stress cause people to release stress hormones such as cortisol, which are beneficial in the short-term and could enhance the immune system? Or is it the improvement in mood after several days of writing that brings the benefits for immunity? So far, no one knows.

But no matter how it works, journaling is a great way to process your emotions by writing about things you don't feel comfortable talking about, to reflect on your experiences and process emotions, to construct a more coherent story of what is happening, and to explore other perspectives of the same story. Expressive writing can also help process your feelings and maybe having this outlet can give you a better sense of control over your feelings. In writing, our complex brains and our complicated lives can come together in meaningful ways, and we can come up with insights that we could not have predicted in advance.

In conclusion, expressive writing is no panacea, it shows moderate effects and, as many of the psychological techniques, it works better for some people than others. However, given the evidence so far, it is reasonable to conclude that could be beneficial, even if it is for the short term. If you want to give expressive writing a try and see whether it works for you, the box contains some prompts to guide you.

Expressive writing prompts originated by J. Pennebaker

- Write for 20 minutes.
- Choose a topic extremely personal and important to you. Although several variations on the expressive writing method have been tested, none are consistently superior to the original method that encourages participants to freely choose their writing topic. Don't focus on the writing itself but on your chosen topic and the role of your emotions in the overall story.
- Type or handwritten is fine. Although no studies have compared ways of writing on health outcomes, a few have explored if the mode of writing can influence people's ratings of the expressive writing procedure itself.

There is some evidence[19] that writing by hand produced more negative affect and led to more self-rated disclosure than did typing. One possibility is that writing by hand is slower and encourages individuals to process their thoughts and feelings more deeply.

- **Write continuously.** Do not worry about punctuation, spelling and grammar. If you run out of things to say, it's OK to repeat the previous line. Keep the pen on paper or fingers on the keyboard.
- **Write only for yourself.** This exercise is for your eyes only.
- **If you get into the writing, and you feel you cannot write about a particular event because it pushes you over the edge, STOP writing!**

Responding to the illness

But if we can mitigate the impact of the condition, why is not everyone doing it? Because we have different opportunities, we come from diverse backgrounds and we respond differently to life challenges. According to King's Fund[14] report on self management of long term conditions, people have different approaches to illness management. For example, one of the people they interviewed for the report, Bill, a 79-year-old with chronic obstructive pulmonary disease, did not want information about his condition; he did not want to discuss his care anymore than he needed to. When describing one of his regular visits to the hospital, he said:

They take your blood, there's no discussion, they're too busy, just a bloke with a machine. Then the nurse tells you there's no change this time, which things haven't altered. I don't want to know more. The GP – we work together – he tells me what to do – but he's the doctor, that's what he gets paid for.

For Bill, management of his condition will continue to be what the doctor decides and does. By contrast, Debbie, in her mid-20s and diagnosed with diabetes, came around slowly to the idea that she had to live with it and took a more active role in managing her diabetes:

[I was] searching on the internet and found Diabetes UK. It took a while to sink in. I was too frightened to find out, [and I] didn't know the GP or nurse at the time. I felt like I was stupid, then I was in denial. It took me a long time to get to grips with it. There is an education day at the hospital, [and I've been] waiting for ages to get referred to the hospital that runs this.

Debbie is not the only one who takes this approach to deal with her condition. For a lot of people, receiving the diagnosis is very frightening and confusing. However, research studies that follow up people with long-term conditions for some time show that over time a lot of people will eventually accept their health status and regain a psychological equilibrium. We are much more resilient than we think and as the cliché goes, we are not given what we can't handle. Researchers now are trying to understand those inner resources better and work out how best to use them.

There is a lot to be said about acceptance and the role it plays in adjusting to physical illnesses. Studies have shown that even if we take into consideration illness variables and other demographic and social factors, people who report higher acceptance also feel happier and report less severe symptoms.[15] Acceptance is usually recognised as the first step in processing and dealing with the condition. The illness feels like the unpleasant uninvited guest to your party. It comes and does not want to leave no matter how hard you are trying to push it out of the door. You will be angry at this guest, you will sit in a corner waiting for them to go, you will try with all your might to ignore them and ignore the mess they are making, but the guest will be there, unpleasant and ever present. With acceptance, what we are trying to do is create some room for this guest. You give them a place of their own, they can sit there and make less mess in the rest of the house, and you will have more space around them to enjoy your party food, party games and all your other guests. The unpleasant guest will be at your party, you will tend to them, but you will also enjoy the rest of the party despite their presence.

Accepting means simply allowing space for whatever is going on, rather than trying to create some other state. Through acceptance, we settle back into awareness of what is present. We let it be – we merely notice and observe whatever is already present.

Accepting difficulties is not resignation – resignation is passive; acceptance allows us, as a vital step, to become fully aware of problems, and then, if appropriate, to respond skilfully rather than to react by automatically running some of our old (and maybe unhelpful) strategies for dealing with difficulties.

Acceptance may often be the first step of skilful action that leads
to positive change. However, there are also situations that might be
very difficult, or actually impossible, to change. In this case, there is
the danger that, by carrying on, trying to solve an insoluble problem, or by refusing to accept the reality of the situation we are in,
we may end up exhausting ourselves and increasing our sense of
helplessness.[16] In practice the more we try to control certain things
the more uncontrollable they may become. It will undoubtedly be
impossible to control symptoms all of the time.

But, how do people arrive at the point of acceptance? Is acceptance what comes first before people start making adjustments
in their lives or does it happen after people begin accommodating
their condition? Is acceptance something that happens to everyone
and for all illnesses? What happens after people arrive at the place
of acceptance? Is acceptance something that occurs once and stays
or something we need to work on to sustain? This last question is
especially relevant for conditions that are progressing over time.

Psychologists have studied these questions, and they identified
a phenomenon called *response shift*. *Response shift* refers to the
improved reports people make on their quality of life and their
symptoms the longer they have the condition.[17] Researchers believe
that this shift in people's perceptions of their condition happens
because people reprioritise and change their values, internal standards and their attitudes of illness. Someone who has developed
chronic back pain may feel it's getting worse initially, and they
may have difficulties keeping up with household chores and work.
If the same person is asked the same questions after initial treatment attempts, they will report that their disability and pain are
worse now than they were in the beginning. In other words, even
if the objective symptoms have improved after the initial attempts
of treatment, their internal standards of pain have changed. They
compare their current pain with how they felt before the problem appeared. However, over time, even if the treatment attempts
did not improve the objective measure of pain, they perceive the
pain as less severe and interfering. People are likely to take a more
holistic view of their condition. They have re-conceptualised their
symptoms as localised back pain in the context of an otherwise
well and pain-free body, thus changing the meaning and impact of
their pain.

Response shift was initially noticed and studied in educational
research in the 1970s, where investigators saw students' internal

standards of competency changed as a result of learning more about the subject. For example, students rated their abilities or knowledge in a particular area as stronger or better until they learned more about it. When they've learned more, they rated their skills as less or the same as before they started learning. Similarly, people with pain may rate themselves as more disabled after treatment than they did before because the yardstick has changed.

It turns out we appraise our health condition in harsher tones after the diagnosis since we compare our current health with the pre-diagnosis self. Given some time we adapt to new circumstances, and we arrange our intrinsic values, processes and standards in a way that is protective of our psychological and physical well-being.

The turning point

Blanche

Blanche said she was the perfect candidate to get this condition. She had a theory that you grow into the illness that fits you. She always considered her time precious and she did not like to waste any of it on trivialities. She loved doing things she thoroughly enjoyed or things that made her feel productive and nothing in between. Now she is even more careful with how she spends her time and energy. Blanche kept up her usual activities, only now she works at the shop fewer hours. She does something outside of the house nearly every day – she hates staying in the house all day. Her diary gets filled up very quickly as she is a board member of the learning and development committee at her daughters' school and also a board member of the youth engagement committee for her church. However, she can no longer attend more than a meeting a day because of her fatigue. She has also changed the focus of her involvement. She only attends committee meetings that take place at the school, and she has switched to coordinating events, avoiding hands-on tasks. In her free time, she reads research developments related to her condition online. She never did much work around the house, and this is still the case. But she likes inventing games for her daughters and taking her family out to museums and galleries. She figures it is best to spend her limited energy on her children and husband rather than doing house chores that she loathes.

Her social life has remained the same, only now her friends come around to her place, where she feels more comfortable and relaxed. Her friends know about her condition. So, when she gets tired, or her body starts to ache, she can 'kick them out'- as she puts it with a loud laugh.

But it is not all plain sailing; she gets sad from time to time that she can no longer do the things she used to be able to do. When she goes on holidays with her husband to Tenerife, a beloved summer destination, they are not able to walk by the sea as much as they used. Occasionally, she also feels mild panic. When she feels panicky, she does mindful breathing that she learnt at her 6-week self-management course or tries to distract herself by thinking of other things.

It took her some time, but she has now a good relationship with her health care team. She's undertaking a program of graded exercises that she reviews with her physiotherapist monthly. An occupational therapist has assessed her needs and advised her on ways to reserve energy. She has a very distinct and definite idea of what she wants from the medical team, and she gets it.

Blanche manages a very full life even when she feels like there are two 3-year-olds attached to her legs. Over time, Myalgic Encephalitis has fallen into the background, and the focus now is on continuing her life.

There was a turning point in Blanche's journey. Once she finally had the diagnosis and prognosis of her condition, she shifted her attention to things she could do to manage it. Blanche thought it was best to outsmart her condition, rather than battle it heads on. She took up the self-management course that her doctor had suggested. It was based on compassion-based therapy. The course taught her to listen to her needs and be kind to her body. It was a very gentle approach and something in stark contrast to how she previously operated. The group element of that course made her feel uncomfortable, initially. She was not one to share her troubles with strangers, but soon she settled in the group and found the idea of being kind to one's body intriguing. Blanche realised how harshly she was judging herself. During the meditation practices in the course, she noticed many self-criticisms coming into her mind again and again. Protective and caring to her family, friends and colleagues, she never really directed this care towards herself.

While for some people and some conditions the turning point comes once they have the name of their condition and know the prognosis or when they have identified the right medications, for others, it takes more time.

But how and when does this turning point happen? When do the uncertainty and fear settle, and we can switch gears to getting control of the symptoms? It will be different for everyone. It depends on our personality, coping style, social circumstances and, of course, the illness itself.

Blanche found new ways to cope with her condition and deal with her symptoms. She discovered the means to carry on doing the things she loved only after she had made peace with her diagnosis and the fact that there is not a straightforward treatment. Eventually, we find ways to balance things out and adopt the routines that work best for us.

In my research, I explore what helps people accommodate their condition while retaining the essence of who they are. In research interviews people often say that a 'turning point' came after months or even years of trying to ignore symptoms and carrying on as usual, or of always thinking about the condition and how bad it might get. People talk about reaching a point where they realise that they can't carry on like this anymore. They need to let go; they need to change the course of action because things are not working.

But is it possible to get to that point quicker? What if you can direct your attention back to the things you used to love? What if you can improve your health – because you are managing stress, sleeping well, eating well and moving your body, always gently and respecting its limits – and you find the energy and the time to help others?

What if you can have enough energy to get reacquainted with your partner, both as lovers and friends, not just as a carer and patient discussing medical appointments and treatments and hashing out logistics of care plans? And what if you can do all this – *and* tend to your garden, or paint, or whatever else you secretly desire – without longing about a magic cure that will make everything easy again?

The hard – but hopeful – truth is that you can. Yes, you have a lot going on in your life. You may be wondering whether you will be able to read this book while you are in pain or your mind feels fuzzy after a few pages. But before you put it down to have a break, I want to make sure you take away two thoughts: *you can manage your condition so it influences your life less* and *you have more strength than you think.*

When the body is not working, we don't think about how to have a fulfilling life, and we spend most of our time trying to deal with the condition. Having a long-term condition is overwhelming, and it fills all our time. It is only natural; how can you think about leisure and nurturing relationships when you are always in pain or depleted of energy? When making a cup of tea is a major operation that takes half an hour? We spend very little time on things that require more thought or initiative, like playing with our kids, exercising, or engaging in projects that align with who we are and what we want to achieve in life. We squeeze these activities out while the condition takes more and more of our time and more space in our mind. And consequently, we feel overwhelmed by the condition and are underprepared for the task of managing it all.

Oliver

Oliver was a personal tutor. He lived on the outskirts of London, but he travelled to London frequently to meet his pupils. He also loved exercising and being out in nature. Last spring, it was a busy period with his work and had to travel a lot into London. At that time, he started noticing pain in his left shoulder and stiffness at his neck. He was also feeling more tired than usual. He thought the pain and the fatigue were due to stress and lack of exercise and once the exams period for his students was over, he would sort things out.

But one day, while helping one of his pupils on an assignment on Parkinson's disease, it occurred to him that maybe he had Parkinson's. Due to his age and level of fitness, he did not believe it to be true but made an appointment with his GP, who referred him to a neurologist, who confirmed that he did indeed have early onset Parkinson's disease. Even though he knew Parkinson's is not fatal; he started thinking a lot about his mortality. He lost interest in everything. His GP worried about his emotional well-being and referred him to a psychotherapist.

Working with the psychotherapist for a little more than a year opened new doors for him. First of all, he reframed his fears of dying. He realised it was time to take stock of his life and decide what he wanted to do, as this could be the last active chapter of his life. He was not forcing himself to be cheerful with Parkinson's or put on a brave face, but he felt at peace with having this condition.

Oliver has found a way to live well with his condition. It did not happen automatically, and he needed some help. It took Oliver a couple of years to come to the realisations described here and more time was necessary for him to arrange things in a way that aligned with his needs.

I will not pretend this is easy. To live well with their condition, people said they had to attend many medical appointments, learn more about their condition, change jobs, cut down their working hours, move houses, reassess their friendships and their relationships in their families. In other words, they had to take a holistic approach to attend their symptoms. In this book, I'll talk about how to make these changes in a gradual way that respects your limits and needs. A lot of people know that they need to change things, but the gap between their current state and the one they wish to achieve seems so significant that they feel overwhelmed and are dreading making even a small step.

The best way to start on living well when feeling unwell – and get the most out of this book – is to make an itinerary of what has changed and what is challenging now. Identify the symptoms that get most in the way of you doing what you want to do, like a researcher or a clinician that records symptoms with an objective eye.

Be as mindful as you can, starting with the diagnosis. What did the doctor say about your condition? What are the symptoms? What happens as soon as you wake up in the morning? What about when you want to have a shower and breakfast? How do you feel before taking your medication and how do you feel after? How much of your time is spent feeling energised and alert and how much tired or worn out? Which days and times do you feel more tired? How many breaks do you need when making dinner? Why do you need breaks? Is it pain, or dizziness, or lack of strength? If you are exercising, how does it affect you? How many times a day do you have to remember to do something related to the condition, for example, take a pill, inject insulin, check your blood pressure? I'm giving a lot of examples here not to confuse you or to think that you need to go into this analysis paralysis for every single thing in your life, but to show you that you need to have details of what it is happening before you attempt to fix it. The next chapters will cover more about what to do with the things you have identified, how to best manage the symptoms and find ways to adjust activities.

Once we know what has changed exactly, we can then decide what things to let go of and what to amend. Listing your limitations and challenges might temporarily bring you down, but eventually, it will empower you. It is essential that you feel supported to manage your overall health and well-being. These challenges do not rule your life. They are issues that need solving. Once you are clear about symptoms and problems you are experiencing and you would like to address, you can have a care plan discussion with your health care team or doctor. Personalised care planning aims to encourage people with long-term conditions to select treatment goals and to work with clinicians to determine their specific needs for treatment and support.[18] In England, 72% of people with long-term conditions use their care plan to manage everyday health.[19]

There are many good and not-so-good reasons to change your plans when they stop serving you. Nonetheless, it is a choice you need to make, acutely aware of consequences. Maybe you carry on working because you think it is worth persevering, perhaps you choose to quit because you don't enjoy what you do anymore, or perhaps you can't decide what to do. You don't have to have all the answers and make all the decisions now. Thinking 'this is my choice' puts you back in control. This is something you need to deal with; no one else can do this for you. It is your life, and you live it the way you want to live it.

How to start your itinerary

The key to success in any undertaking is first, deciding what you want to do; second, determining how you are going to do it; and finally, learning a set of skills and practising them until they have been mastered. It helps to make things as specific as possible not only to get a more objective view of how things are and avoid the halo effect (the tendency for an impression created in one area to influence opinion in another area) but also as a first step to live with intention.

For simplicity, let's categorise events into enjoyable and frustrating. Think of yesterday's events in as much detail as possible and fill in the provided tables.

Enjoyable events

What happened yesterday? Go over everything that you did. Which activities did you enjoy the most? Did you lose track of time and if yes, what did you do? What put a smile on your face?

Events	Thoughts and emotions
e.g. I woke up early even though I no longer work on Fridays.	I felt relief that I now have a day a week just for me. I put together a list of things I want to do on Fridays.

Events	Thoughts and emotions
My husband brought me a cup of tea in bed in the afternoon.	I felt grateful but also sad thinking of how much I'll miss him next week when he'll be away with work.

Frustrating events

What are the things you would have liked to be different? Was there anything that you found overwhelming, stressful, frustrating or distressing?

Events	Thoughts and Emotions
e.g. I forgot to take my medication.	I felt frustration and worry, I thought that something must be wrong with me to keep forgetting.

Events	Thoughts and Emotions
Stiffness on my shoulders in the morning.	I felt isolated, alone, not valued. They have not invited me because I'd be in their way and they wouldn't be able to do what they wanted to do.

Looking back at both of these tables, what do you notice? Can you spot any patterns? Is one table busier than the other? Some people find it challenging to identify thoughts and emotions that accompany events. If this is true for you, don't give up. You will become better with practice. Initially you might notice thoughts that are more persistent and come up again and again but as you practice you will be able to identify more subtle thoughts that make a brief appearance.

If yesterday was not a typical day, you can choose to do this exercise using a different day, or even keep an enjoyable/frustrating diary for a week to see how things change from day to day.

Pause for reflection

- What aspects of my condition do I find difficult to accept? How could I open up and allow them to be in my life?
- How did I find the expressive writing exercise? Is it worth pursuing?
- What is my self-management style? Are there any changes I want to make?

Bibliography

1 NHS England. *House of Care: A Framework for Long Term Condition Care*. www.england.nhs.uk/ourwork/clinical-policy/ltc/house-of-care/. Accessed December 30, 2018.

2 Lorig K, Holman H, Sobel D, Laurent D. *Living a Healthy Life with Chronic Conditions: Self-Management of Heart Disease, Arthritis, Diabetes, Depression, Asthma, Bronchitis, Emphysema, and Other Physical and Mental Health Conditions*. Bull Publishing Company; 4th edition, Boulder, CO, USA, 2012.

3 Herbert TB, Cohen S. Depression and Immunity: A Meta-Analytic Review. *Psychological Bulletin*. 1993;113(3):472–486. doi:10.1037/0033-2909.113.3.472

4 Gold SM, Irwin MR. Depression and Immunity: Inflammation and Depressive Symptoms in Multiple Sclerosis. *Immunology and Allergy Clinics of North America*. 2009;29(2):309–320. doi:10.1016/J.IAC.2009.02.008

5 Leserman J. Role of Depression, Stress, and Trauma in HIV Disease Progression. *Psychosomatic Medicine*. 2008;70(5):539–545. doi:10.1097/PSY.0b013e3181777a5f

6 Merolli M, Gray K, Martin-Sanchez F. Health Outcomes and Related Effects of Using Social Media in Chronic Disease Management: A Literature Review and Analysis of Affordances. *Journal of Biomedical Informatics*. 2013;46(6):957–969. doi:10.1016/j.jbi.2013.04.010

7 Pennebaker JW. *Writing to Heal: A Guided Journal for Recovering from Trauma & Emotional Upheaval.* New Harbinger Publications; 2004.

8 Pennebaker JW, Beall SK. Confronting a Traumatic Event: Toward an Understanding of Inhibition and Disease. *Journal of Abnormal Psychology*. 1986;95(3):274–281. doi:10.1037/0021-843X.95.3.274

9 Stanton AL, Danoff-Burg S, Sworowski LA, et al. Randomized, Controlled Trial of Written Emotional Expression and Benefit Finding in Breast Cancer Patients. *Journal of Clinical Oncology*. 2002;20(20): 4160–4168. doi:10.1200/JCO.2002.08.521

10 Zhou C, Wu Y, An S, Li X. Effect of Expressive Writing Intervention on Health Outcomes in Breast Cancer Patients: A Systematic Review and Meta-Analysis of Randomized Controlled Trials. Ozakinci G, ed. *PLoS One*. 2015;10(7):e0131802. doi:10.1371/journal.pone.0131802

11 Frattaroli J. Experimental Disclosure and Its Moderators: A Meta-Analysis. *Psychological Bulletin*. 2006;132(6):823–865. doi:10.1037/0033-2909.132.6.823

12 Robinson H, Jarrett P, Vedhara K, Broadbent E. The Effects of Expressive Writing before or after Punch Biopsy on Wound Healing. *Brain, Behavior, and Immunity*. 2017;61:217–227. doi:10.1016/j.bbi.2016.11.025

13 Pennebaker JW. Putting Stress into Words: Health, Linguistic, and Therapeutic Implications. *Behaviour Research and Therapy*. 1993; 31(6):539–548. www.ncbi.nlm.nih.gov/pubmed/8347112. Accessed December 30, 2018.

14 Corben S, Rosen R. *Self-Management for Long-Term Conditions: Patients' Perspectives on the Way Ahead-Sara Corben, Rebecca Rosen: The King's Fund, 26th July 2005.*; 2003. www.kingsfund.org.uk. Accessed December 30, 2018.

15 Pakenham KI, Fleming M. Relations between Acceptance of Multiple Sclerosis and Positive and Negative Adjustments. *Psychology & Health*. 2011;26(10):1292–1309. doi:10.1080/08870446.2010.517838

16 Segal ZV, Williams JMG, Teasdale JD. *Mindfulness-Based Cognitive Therapy for Depression: A New Approach to Preventing Relapse.* Guilford Press; 2002.

17 Sprangers MA, Schwartz CE. Integrating Response Shift into Health-Related Quality of Life Research: A Theoretical Model. *Social Science & Medicine*. 1999;48(11):1507–1515. www.ncbi.nlm.nih.gov/pubmed/10400253. Accessed December 29, 2018.

18 Reuben DB, Tinetti ME. Goal-Oriented Patient Care: An Alternative Health Outcomes Paradigm. *New England Journal of Medicine.* 2012;366(9):777–779. doi:10.1056/NEJMp1113631
19 Brewin CR, Lennard H. Effects of Mode of Writing on Emotional Narratives. *Journal of Traumatic Stress.* 1999;12(2):355–361. doi:10.1023/ A:1024736828322

Chapter 2

Personal values

Values are your guiding principles. Your values are the qualities that you want to present to the world. They are the foundations of who you are. Why would we bother to step out of our comfort zone to do something different? What's our motivation? What matters enough that we would be willing to go through the trouble of changing things? If we lose touch with our values, we lose our motivation. Think about values that resonate with you and avoid being side-tracked by others' standards and values. You are a unique human being after all, and no one else can do the things you can do or think the way you do. Values are those things that you come back to, which tell you that your life is going in the right direction. The number of values that you have is not relevant. What is important is that you know what they are. They can change as your life changes.

The psychotherapist Carl Rogers, in his book *On becoming a person*[1] talks about the process that takes place for a person to meet his/her full potential and lead a meaningful life. He argues that to come closer to who we are and what we enjoy and to create a joyful life, we should look less to others for approval or disapproval, for standards to live by, for decisions and choices. We recognise that it rests with us to choose, that the only question that matters is 'Am I living in a way that is deeply satisfying to me, and which truly expresses me?'. This, he thinks, is the most crucial question.[1] Identifying your personal values is a way of efficiently re-directing energy and attention to meaningful activities.

Clive

Clive had an athletic build and a warm and friendly look in his eyes. He was living with Eleanor, his wife of 57 years, initially in

Scotland. When Eleanor was pregnant with their first child, they left Scotland for the United States. The move was very stressful for them both. They did not have a plan and did not know anyone in the US, but Clive believed this step was the best choice for his family. Clive worked as a police officer and with Eleanor, they built a beautiful home for their two daughters.

Always proactive and energetic, Clive wanted to stay as healthy as he could for the sake of his family. That was his way of making things easier for them. In his 60s he was also diagnosed with COPD (Chronic Obstructive Pulmonary Disease) and was treated for prostate cancer.

Clive had a full and exciting life, despite the adjustment he had to make and despite the frequent hospital appointments and fatigue that slowed him down. He knew what he wanted to achieve and reacted accordingly without letting others dictate what he should or shouldn't be doing. He tried not to worry about potential obstacles when he wanted to do something; he'd find a way around them.

But things were not always like that. When Clive was younger, working hard and achieving things was something that he valued. He had colleagues and other people validating whether he was working hard or adding value. When he retired, he didn't have this anymore. Initially, it was disorienting. There was no map to follow, no external benchmarks. He had to figure out his own chosen path.

A local hospice organised a seminar on positive thinking that he attended. After the seminar, he chatted with some people who worked there and before leaving the premises he volunteered himself to help with the exercise classes every Saturday morning. It was only a few hours once a week, but he felt he was achieving something significant, he learned new things and met people who also dealt with health issues and that helped him to get some perspective.

The key for Clive was to identify what made him happy and what were the personal qualities he most wanted to express in this area of his life. His past experiences shaped the way he copes with his health issues. His work has taught him to anticipate risks and plan accordingly. He managed to strike a balance between looking after his health while engaging in significant-for-him activities.

From interviewing people who described a fulfilling life while attending to their long-term condition, I understand that these people focus, as much as possible, on things that give them joy and spend some of their time helping others in some capacity. They identify elements from the past that made them happy and rekindle with old hobbies. Assisting others also makes them feel of value. This takes the focus off their situation and directs their attention to others. For Blanche, these two areas were leading others and staying connected to her community. For Clive, it was spending two hours every Saturday to facilitate an exercise class that moved him more towards connectivity. People who live well are the ones who have made peace with their condition, have attended their needs and dreams and then reached out to help others. No fanfare and dramatic changes are needed. Small every day actions will bring the greatest change.

A long-term condition is a bundle of tasks and challenges to take on. There are always things you need to do to manage symptoms like fatigue and pain, to cooperate with health professionals, to manage your family and friends. And life goes on, you have house chores to handle, to arrange for builders to fix that leak in the roof and remember to buy new toothpaste. There are also the social life and obligations you need to consider, buy presents for your auntie's 80th birthday, remember to call your mum to ask about the doctor's appointment, arrange to go out for drinks with friends. The list goes on. Sometimes you may feel on top of things and sometimes overwhelmed. This is not a sign of failure or weakness. It is part of the process of adapting to a long-term condition. Sometimes, you manage your condition actively, and sometimes you take a step back because life gets in the way, the illness changes, life happens.

Some tasks, like sleeping, eating and taking your medication are required, but the rest are merely combinations of choices each of us makes. Identifying your personal values is a way of efficiently redirecting energy and attention to meaningful activities.

It is very simplistic to assume that people with the most severe symptoms will have the most difficulties in finding ways to manage their symptoms and consequently find ways to lead a meaningful life. Studies show that people with the most severe symptoms have preserved their quality of life and positive mood.[2] There are other factors unrelated to the disease, or its direct functional limitations, that explain well-being. Psychological factors, like beliefs about the illness, sense of skillful control over symptoms or ability to process emotional reactions come to play when we have to adjust with severe challenges and changes.[3] Before we unpack these factors in the following chapters, let's start with the basics. What motivates you to make adjustments?

Managing a long-term condition requires a lot of trial and error, perseverance and practice. Values can help you sustain your motivation towards better management of the condition and making life full and meaningful. Hayes and Lillis,[4] clinical psychologists and researchers, described personal values as independent of social approval, external outcomes and sources of negative reinforcement. Negative reinforcement is when a behaviour is strengthened by avoiding a negative or aversive outcome. For example, you eat salad with your dinner (behaviour) to avoid nagging from your partner (negative outcome). When it comes to personal values, regardless of the result of an action, we can always find satisfaction just because the effort is consistent with our values. You eat salad with your dinner because this is consistent with your value of leading a healthy lifestyle. Importantly, the valued actions do not have to be large. It is small steps on a day-to-day basis that work best.

When you take care of your highest values and the most important things first, your life overall is more meaningful, and you will feel calmer and more balanced. According to psychologists Barbara Markway and Celia Ampel in *The Self-Confidence Workbook*[5] values "are principles that give our lives meaning and allow us to persevere through adversity". Values stand for our most meaningful ideals, and also, they inspire us to keep going when things get tough.

Personal values and motivation to change

The concept of personal values and the idea of motivation that comes from within (intrinsic motivation) have been explored in the context of managing long-term conditions. For example, studies have consistently found that people with diabetes are more likely to adhere to a diabetes regime when they believe that the management of their condition is down to their efforts and abilities rather than luck or fate. Also, people were more likely to maintain diet and test blood glucose when they did so because it was consistent with their personal goals.[6] It is easier to carry on your physiotherapy exercises when you want to keep fit so that you spend more time with your children, rather than doing your physiotherapy exercises because your doctor said so and you feel you need to oblige. In the second scenario, you are more likely to only stick with the physiotherapy for a short period. A little while later you will find various excuses not to do them. There has to be something bigger behind you wanting to make changes.

All this evidence about intrinsic motivation (motivation that comes from our personal goals) and personal values can be translated to guide your journey to living well with a long-term health condition. There is no point in putting time and effort into managing your health and changing your lifestyle if this does not open up space in your life for things that are significant to you. Thinking back, could you identify a meaningful moment you lived? What made that moment special, what was it about that moment that made it so memorable? Who were you with, what did you do? How did you feel? What does this moment represent? Think about the motivation that drove to this moment or the sense that surrounded this moment rather than the outcome or the achievement.

Clive, for example, did not talk about how successful he was with volunteering at the exercise classes or helping his family go through tough times. The personal value for Clive was feeling connected with others. It was vital for him to recognise the worth of other people. Show others that he values them through his small everyday actions and his comments. He appreciated spending time with his family. He valued being deeply involved with a group that has a larger purpose beyond himself. He made sure he devoted enough time to activities that either showed respect to other people or made him feel deeply connected to his family and community.

Broadly, those who get the most out of life try to figure out and focus on activities aligned with their values. They know that to have a life with a long-term condition and not just an existence, they fill the space that illness spares them with honing meaningful activities. Better managing of the illness will mean more space for these significant activities.

So what are these personal values? In other words, what would you most like to be doing during the spaces that the illness leaves free and unobstructed?

Some people are blessed to know this from a very early age. Most don't. Some people find out only after they have been diagnosed with a long-term condition. The change, challenge and difficulty that a long-term condition brings can encourage us to ask ourselves some profound questions – what do I personally most want to be about? What qualities do I most want to express in my daily actions? Even if you have a good idea, you might not see all the possibilities that tap into those values, so it helps to spend time finding your own value compass. Most people wouldn't know what their personal values are. We live our lives without really reflecting and examining why we act the way we do, what makes us happy and what gives us pleasure. We are too busy just getting by and doing the things that need doing. This is especially true when you have a long-term condition.

For the moment, put the condition and its challenges aside. We will first look into what makes a life worth living and meaningful for you. Then in the next chapters we will start exploring ways to manage the different challenges you might have identified in the first chapter to create space to focus on the activities that make a life well lived. Having identified your personal values and how you want to spend your life best will hopefully motivate you through your journey of managing your symptoms. Then you will know why you are putting in the effort. You will keep going even when there are setbacks or the condition changes or when there are relapses because you will have a bigger plan for how you want to live your life.

Kate

> Kate loved to write short stories; she liked writing after work and on the weekends. But now her cognitive fatigue was preventing her from concentrating long enough to write. For her birthday, her daughter bought her a colouring book for adults. It was a book with exotic birds, and in the evenings, she loved sitting by her window and choosing colours for the birds and their tropical surroundings. In the end, there were some free pages in the book, and she started doodling. Doodling was easy. Then she started colouring in her doodles, and soon she began to create visual stories. She wasn't writing anymore, but she found a way to tell stories that she found satisfying and yet less cognitively taxing. She realised that she could still move towards expressing the quality of creativity, just in a different way in her daily life.

The solution seemed to have appeared to Kate by chance. But there is a great deal we can do to nudge our luck. First of all, knowing what you like to do and what the personal value is behind it. Why do you love doing something that you feel is important? It is also important to recognise when something has become too much trouble and is no fun anymore. When you are on the lookout for something fun but manageable, it is easier to grab any opportunity that comes your way that fits the bill. Recognising this requires changing the narrative. Instead of saying to yourself 'I can't do X, Y, or Z', you can say 'I am not able to do X, Y, or Z because they are not right for me right now'.

Identifying personal values

To start off identifying your personal values, choose a behaviour or something you regularly do, or you used to do. For example, working hard. Then you need to ask questions to identify why you do what you do, or you did what you did, and you repeat the questions replacing the initial behaviour with the first answer and then the second response and so on until you can't think of anything else.

Taking our example of working hard, ask: what does working so hard give me that is important for me? Perhaps the answer would be so I can make money. The next question would be: what does earning money give me that is important? It could be that I can provide for my family. Then ask: what does providing for my family give me that is important for me? The answer could be they are happy and safe. Next ask: what does having a happy and secure family give me that is important for me? A possible answer for this would be, it gives me peace of mind.

In this example, peace of mind is what's important and is, therefore, a personal value. By recognising this, you can avoid some of the set behaviours such as fear and being overwhelmed by working hard. You can choose to go straight to peace of mind by identifying what will give you peace of mind, which is far more useful.

Go through this strategy for yourself on different examples from your life and with every answer ask "what does X give me that is important for me?" do this until you are unable to find further answers, at this point, you have identified your personal value.

Professor Steven Hayes, one of the founders of Acceptance and Commitment Therapy, suggests that you uncover your values by naming your heroes. For example, why do you admire, say, Mahatma Gandhi? Is it because he fought for social justice? Is it his commitment to non-violence? His kindness to others? Identify the specific values embodied by your heroes can inspire you to adopt those values for yourself.

Another useful exercise on values was developed by business coach John Assaraf which will help you to connect with what you value most in your life. Start by writing down all the things you value in your life. Some examples could be things like health, time, freedom, creativity, love, fun or peace. Then select your most important and put them in order from one to ten, where one has the highest value.

There are hundreds of different values and not all of them will be relevant to you. There are no right or wrong values. It's like your taste; some people like cherry cola, some people prefer lime with soda. It's not that cherry cola is better than lime soda, it's just that different people prefer different things.

Dr Russ Harris, the author of The *Happiness Trap*,[7] has generously provided free online resources on how to identify personal values, as well as a list of values and their definitions to help you identify more. Here are some example values to get you started:

A	B	C	D	E
Abundance	Balance	Calmness	Daring	Eagerness
Acceptance	Beauty	Camaraderie	Decisiveness	Economy
Accessibility	Being the best	Candour	Decorum	Ecstasy
Accomplishment	Belonging	Capability	Deference	Education
Accuracy	Benevolence	Caring	Delight	Effectiveness
Achievement	Bliss	Carefulness	Democracy	Efficient
Acknowledgement	Boldness	Celebrity	Dependability	Elation
Activeness	Bravery	Certainty	Depth	Elegance
Adaptability	Brilliance	Challenge	Desire	Empathy
Adoration		Change	Determination	Encouragement
Advancement		Charity	Devotion	Endurance
Adventure		Cheerfulness	Devoutness	Energy

F	G	H	I	J
Fairness	Gallantry	Happiness	Imagination	Joy
Faith	Generosity	Harmony	Impact	Judiciousness
Fame	Gentility	Health	Impartiality	Justice
Family	Giving	Heart	Independence	
Fascination	Grace	Helpfulness	Industry	
Fashion	Gratitude	Heroism	Ingenuity	
Fearlessness	Gregariousness	Holiness	Inquisitiveness	
Ferocity	Growth	Honesty	Insightfulness	
Fidelity	Guidance	Honour	Inspiration	
Fierceness		Hopefulness	Integrity	
Financial		Hospitality	Intelligence	
independence		Humility	Intensity	
Fitness				

(Continued)

(Continued)

K	L	M	N	O
Keenness	Leadership	Majesty	Neatness	Obedience
Kindness	Learning	Making a difference	Nerve	Open-mindedness
Knowledge	Liberation	Mastery		Openness
	Liberty	Maturity		Optimism
	Liveliness	Meaning		Order
	Logic	Meekness		Organisation
	Longevity	Mellowness		Originality
	Love	Merit		Outlandishness
	Loyalty	Meticulousness		Outrageousness
		Mindfulness		
		Modesty		
		Motivation		

P	Q	R	S	T
Passion	Quirky	Realism	Sacredness	Teamwork
Patience		Reason	Sacrifice	Temperance
Peace		Reasonableness	Safety	Thankfulness
Perceptiveness		Recognition	Sagacity	Thoroughness
Perfection		Recreation	Saintliness	Thrift
Perkiness		Reciprocity	Sanguinity	Tidiness
Perseverance		Refinement	Security	Timeliness
Persistence		Reflection	Self-control	Traditionalism
Persuasiveness		Relaxation	Selflessness	Tranquillity
Philanthropy		Reliability	Self-awareness	Transcendence
Physical challenge		Religious-ness	Self-care	Trust
Playfulness		Reputation	Self-development	Trustworthiness
		Resilience	Sympathy	
			Synergy	

U	V	W	X	Y	Z
Understanding	Valour	Warmth		Youthfulness	Zeal
Unflappability	Variety	Watchfulness			
Uniqueness	Victory	Wealth			
Unity	Vigour	Wilfulness			
Usefulness	Virtue	Willingness			
Utility	Vision	Winning			
	Vitality	Wisdom			
	Vivacity	Wittiness			
		Wonder			
		Work alone			
		Work under			
		pressure			
		Work with others			

Mark the personal values that speak most to you and then identify maybe a handful that you think are the most important. Go with your gut. Notice what attracts you the most. Which ones do you feel most motivated to express in your daily life? The question to then ask yourself is: what small things could I do today or tomorrow that might help me move towards expressing my personal value? If for example, you have health first, you would be asking yourself what you could do today to ensure you act upon it. That could be anything from eating healthily to doing some exercise or taking some time out to relax. I'll discuss more ideas in later chapters.

When I tried to identify my five personal values, I found it nearly impossible to narrow them down to five. I thought there were a lot more that were important to me and I could not discard them. My experience is typical; many people when they try this exercise find it nearly impossible to choose from the vast number of values that all look legitimate, but they may not be precisely the ones close to your heart.

One of the common misunderstandings is that we think something is essential for us because either it is something that our society in general or our community in particular values or because we have been told from a very young age that this is the 'right' thing to do. Being diligent, hard-working and dedicated is something valued by our employers, and you get a lot of praise when you are behaving in a way that shows industriousness. Maybe acting lovingly or affectionately towards your family was something that was a 'rule' when you were growing up; your parents showed that to you and your siblings and you were encouraged to show affection and love towards your parents and siblings as well. But, would being loving and being hard-working move you? Is it what you want to stand for in life?

Differentiating between what is important to you and what you have learned through social conditioning can confuse actions with values. The fact that you spend a lot of time helping your parents does not necessarily mean this is a personal value. Would you support them for the sake of helping? Would that fulfil you? Or is it something else hidden that satisfies you? What is it that compels you to spend almost every weekend at their house helping with odds and ends? Maybe it is that through assisting them you feel valued. The more you help, the more valued you feel and this is why you are such a dedicated offspring.

Also, values do make our lives more meaningful and fulfilling but are not always associated with pleasant and happy activities.

For example, looking after your children is essential to you because caring is your personal value. But this does not necessarily mean that looking after your children will always make you feel happy. There will be times that you are far too tired to read the same story to them for the tenth time before bed. But you do carry on reading because it gives you this broad sense of caring that you value.

For committing to anything that will require effort, time, planning and adjustments, it is always a good idea to start off by looking at your personal values and thinking whether or how what you are endeavouring to do aligns (or not) with your personal values. This will not only clarify your motivation, but this knowledge will carry you through when things get tough, when you have a setback or when the symptoms are getting in the way and pulling you down.

Before I started working on this book, I had to connect to my personal values to keep me motivated. Why was I writing this book? What did I want to achieve and how did writing this book align with my personal values? The obvious reasons, like improving my CV and boosting my career, were OK reasons but not important enough for me to commit to this project. *Recognition* and *expertise*, even though very well received in my field and very rewarding values, were not close to my personal values.

After working in academia for more than a decade, it took me a while to separate what were my personal values and the values that are expected in my field. *Learning* stood out for me. I love learning new things and, what better way to deepen your understanding in an area than to write a book about it? To collect and synthesise all the knowledge I had accumulated over the years and push myself to the next level by presenting it in a book format.

But still, it didn't feel like I had hit the right chord. I had many other ways to tap into my *learning* personal value that were less taxing and complex. There was something different behind my drive to write this book. It took me an afternoon, thinking about it, looking over the list of personal values, writing about why I wanted to write and then asking the why question again and again. Why do I want to write? Because I can. But why? To share knowledge and insight. But why? To give me a greater sense of purpose. But why? Because I have something important to share. But why? Because I want to make a difference in people's lives. Then the why's stopped. That was it.

What drives me is making a difference in people's lives. 'Contribution' was my personal value. What drives me is that I want to contribute, help, assist and make a positive difference to others.

That was meaningful for me. Knowing that by writing this book I could, in a small or significant way, help others was what was behind my drive to write the book. It kept me going when life got busy with a new managerial position at work and young children at home. I needed to rearrange a lot of things to make sure I had the time to keep on writing this book. This is what got me out of a writer's block. I wasn't writing out of vanity or to fulfil a career step. I was doing it because it mattered to me. I was writing because I want to make a difference.

Finding the personal value that drives a somewhat contained and time-limited project is one thing. Finding the personal value behind taking charge of your condition is another. As I mentioned in the first chapter, there are a lot of different elements and challenges when managing a long-term condition. Deciding to take more control over the symptoms will initially increase the hassle so you might have to identify more than one personal value that guides you. There might be a value that drives taking better care of your body, e.g. health. Apart from health you also need to identify other personal values that will encourage you to enrich your life. So, when your symptoms interfere less with your life, what are you going to do with the freed-up time and energy? What activities will you be doing? How are you going to elevate your every day, such that it does not feel like plain existence but a meaningful life?

While we try to identify values in things we enjoy doing, and we make time to do them even when there are barriers, we can also determine values, through events or actions that are deeply hurtful. Dr Hayes suggests that you learn about your values by thinking back to both the most pleasant and most painful moments of your life. Thinking of these moments could direct you to what you care about most. For instance, if you won an award for a charity volunteering lead, consider that 'leadership' or 'motivating others' might be significant values. What were the most painful experiences? If someone accused you of having mistreated them, and this is deeply troubling to you, that you couldn't stop thinking about it, and you went out of your way trying to rectify it, it might mean that fairness is something that you value more than you thought.

How do you want to spend your time?

To build a more fulfilling and productive life, you have to figure out what you want to be doing with your time, the time that is not spent attending your condition. Life becomes richer when our personal values align with what we do.

Kelly Wilson and Troy DuFrene in their book *Mindfulness for Two*[8] identified 12 life domains that can help you group your values. The 12 domains are:

1 Family (other than couples or parenting)
2 Marriage/couples/intimate relations
3 Parenting
4 Friends/social life
5 Work
6 Education/training
7 Recreation/fun
8 Spirituality
9 Community life
10 Physical self-care (diet/exercise/sleep)
11 The environment (caring for the planet)
12 Aesthetics (art, music, literature, beauty).

Of course, not everyone will have values for all those 12 domains, but I find it useful to consider the multiple facets of life. I tended to think about my values in a binary way, work and personal. Surprisingly, there was minimal overlap of values in this more granular approach. For marriage, the values that I assigned are being a loving, supportive, caring partner. My friendships and social life I like to be driven by fun; I like to be fun-loving and seek, create and engage in fun-filled activities. In my work, I value being orderly, organised and also persistent, to continue resolutely, despite problems or difficulties. Physical self-care is driven by kindness towards myself. I know that if I don't look after myself first, I won't be of any use to anyone else and I won't be able to lead a meaningful life. Therefore, I try to be compassionate, considerate, nurturing and caring towards myself, knowing this will then extend to others. Identifying activities that align with my values in the parenting and aesthetics domain got me excited. The former area is new to me and the latter being neglected. The nice thing about this exercise is that having these different categories as a guide will help you think of your life as a whole.

Try to think about values and domains in life that you would like to focus on, and we will move to actions and goals later on. First of all, you need to narrow the focus and identify the broad motivations. Try to edit as much as you can. There is always the danger to choose all the domains and assign lots of values to each, and this will only confuse things further. Even though you might value a lot of things in life, try focusing for now on your **personal** values, the values that are deeper and more superior than all others. It is essential here to include domains that you have neglected, but that you feel will add meaning to your life.

Olivia

Olivia used to be a playgroup facilitator at her local kindergarten. She loved being around kids, and she loved her job. However, as her Parkinson's disease progressed Olivia was less and less able to run after toddlers, and her employer asked her to resign as she was not fit for her role. She resisted that idea and pleaded with her that she could still do the job, she has experience and kids loved her, she just needed to adjust the games she was playing with the kids, but to no avail. Her employer gave her one month notice to find another more suitable position. She was devastated. She talked to her Parkinson's Disease nurse who directed her to employment advocacy. Olivia did everything she could to keep her job, but she wasn't able to.

After finding herself without a job, she decided to enrol on a psychology course through Open University. She loved the lectures on neuro-psychology and psycho-immunology. She stayed up late looking up things online, she bought all the books the lecturers suggested, and every morning she was excited to make a cup of tea and read one of her books or lecture notes. In the afternoons, she usually spent an hour or two working on the various assignments or revising for exams.

Olivia's real passion, in the end, was learning new things. Knowledge was her personal value. She was genuinely interested in human nature. She was fascinated by science and the human brain. She was thirsty to learn things. Her disability had taken away a job that she valued, but she was able to find her passion and follow it.

Creating a meaningful file

To add new dimensions and more texture in life, it helps to know what motivates you, what makes you tick, what makes you feel fulfilled. Not what others think you should be doing with your time and not what you think you ought to be doing but what you truly want to do. What makes you 'you'.

Using the following spreadsheet (or a notebook, or a document on your computer) write down as many values as you can think of that correspond with how you feel. Writing the values by choosing some from pages 41–42 is fine, but you will get more specific ideas if you also add an activity that you think corresponds with this value. For example, you can either write down 'wonder' or 'wonder, e.g. looking at star configurations'. If you find it challenging to find activities, leave the value blank for the time being and mull over it for the next few days or ask a friend or family member for suggestions. Later on, you can come back and fill in the blanks.

Activities to help you identify your personal values

1 Focusing on you

List as many values from as you think are important to you

- to add clarity, specify activities that align with the value of your choice
- can you spot any patterns or trends on the actions you enjoyed in the past, now and also want to see in the future? Maybe these activities come under the same value.

2 Choose the top three values

Reading back the values you have listed, which one makes you feel really excited? Is there one that you can't wait to get going?

1 _____

2 _____

3 _____

3 Test drive your values

Take yourself back through the last hour, day, week, month or year and ask:

- What choices do I consciously made that move me closer to what I love doing? – remembering that it is all about small everyday actions, not big changes or goals.
- Conversely, what are the choices that I don't make?
- Is what I am doing, or have been doing, bringing me closer or further away to what I love doing?
- What have I done today that energises me, 'what and who do I see looking back?'
- How would others describe me?

Use some of these questions to ask trusted friends and family what they think. Pull out the important points, the repeated words or phrases, look for commonality and difference. What does this tell you?

Translating values into actions

When you know who you are and the brilliant things only you can do, it makes it easier to get out there and be the best version of yourself. Being very clear about who you are and what you stand for will allow you to better connect with your goals and it will be easier to translate your values into actions. Without a direction, you cannot take meaningful and purposeful steps.

Having defined what you like doing and which values motivate your actions, you have started developing a vision of how you'd like your life to look. There is no right format or length. However, the more detailed and specific your idea is, the more connected to you it will be and the easier it will be to set your outcomes or goals.

A personal vision is based on your emotional aspirations, representing a picture of your future. The difficulty is that we do not have full control of the future and this is especially true when you live with a long-term condition. This means that your vision can often creep from being something that is galvanising and motivational to an aspirational picture that is sketchy and challenging to achieve. The challenge is to not only identify how to convert the aspiration into reality but also to review and modify the vision when/if things change both in terms of your condition and your personal priorities.

Choose one of your values and break it down into manageable activities that correspond to this value. If there is one significant activity that corresponds to that value, you can break it down into smaller steps. Each action should take between 15 minutes and 2 hours. And remember, the smaller the step, the easier it is to fit into the day.

Let's assume *wonder* is a motivating force for you. Let's think about the value and what it means. Wonder makes us feel emotionally elevated. It has much in common with awe, but it also overlaps with curiosity. 'Wonder is a state of broad attention in which we feel good and think clearly and connect to phenomena beyond ourselves'.[i]

What we wonder at changes according to circumstances, age and culture. It may be something as apparent as the stars. It may be the fact that every second, billions of neutrinos from the sun are streaming through your body at almost the speed of light. It's up to you to decide what makes you wonder and the list of the activities that you can incorporate in your life that can make you wonder is endless, but I'll attempt a few examples:

- look at the stars and learn the names of a few constellations
- visit a museum
- study a book on physics, botany, geology etc.
- go for a stroll around the nearest park and observe the plants and trees, by really looking at them trying to identify their type, observe their shape, colours and textures; take deep breaths and see if you can describe all the different scents around
- take apart an old radio and try to figure out the role of the various parts, and then try to put it back together.

The list of wonders in nature, science and technology are endless, so I won't go on with examples; I hope you get the idea. Choose activities that won't take too long, and that you can include quite easily in your day, and most of the things in the preceding list can be done flexibly at a time and place that suits you.

On the other hand, you may have something more specific in mind. You might want to learn more about a particular topic or gain a degree. This is a big project, and you need to break it into smaller steps that can fit into your day. For example:

- research courses that best suit you regarding location, format, content (online or in the local college, university or a short course organised by the council)

- make phone calls to inquire about the course
- visit possible colleges
- create a financial plan, if it is a private course you are attending, and you need to save money
- buy notebooks, pens, files folders, organisers
- update software that you will need for the class or get any other equipment you need for the course's homework
- attend the induction day
- arrange a coffee date with a couple of people who have just finished the course.

The smaller the steps, the easier it will be to get started and get going; it will feel less intimidating and you will know what needs to be done each day or each time you'd like to tackle the task. This way you will live each day intentionally according to your values.

Over to you now to make your plan:

1   activities (or steps of a bigger activity) that correspond with
    _____ (add your value)

    1 _____

    2 _____

    3 _____

    4 _____

    5 _____

    6 _____

    7 _____

    8 _____

    9 _____

  10 _____

2   The two activities that I can start with straight away are:

    1 _____

    2 _____

What can get in the way of putting values into action?

The other important step to make sure your aspirational goals become reality is to identify your barriers and ways to overcome them. Obstacles that get in the way of turning your values into action are as unique as you. What we find challenging has very much to do with our circumstances and personal tendencies. It is necessary to think long and hard about what might get in your way. If you anticipate the barrier, it is a thousand times easier to prevent it from appearing or tackle it as soon as it does.

Three common barriers

1 The 'yes . . . but' game

The mind prefers things to stay the same. The mind is a wonderful machine but it likes efficiency and changing things up will require a settling-in period and reconfiguring pathways. So, it will come up with lots of reasons why you can't do certain things. "It's too hard", "No one will take me seriously", "I'm too tired to do anything", "I've tried before and failed", "I'll always fail" and so on. Some of the reasoning might be accurate and based on facts, some on speculations. Try to treat all thoughts like what they are – thoughts. Don't take them personally, they are thoughts and you are more than your thoughts. You can write those thoughts down. It's best to know them, separate them from any emotion and disentangle them from further thoughts. Thoughts that are linked together can quickly escalate to more and more distressing thoughts. They can convince you of their truthfulness even if they are based on assumptions and speculations. Writing them down is one way to let them be but not linger in your mind. Then you can decide on the accuracy of those thoughts. Better yet, you can talk to your partner or a close friend or family member about those thoughts and ask their opinion on the accuracy of the arguments your mind makes against specific actions.

2 The over-achievers trap

This is almost the opposite of the first barrier but is also very common and keeps us from taking action by setting excessive goals or goals that exceed our resources. If you don't get overwhelmed and frozen by those goals, you will probably fail. For an extreme example: to run an ultra-marathon, you need a vast amount of resources: excellent health, brilliant stamina, lots of time to train, excellent social support. Without these resources, you're stuck. Unfortunately, it takes more than enthusiasm and will to accomplish goals and fulfil dreams. Common resources that we might lack are time, health and energy but there are also other hidden resources that we might need such as social support, relevant life skills such as assertiveness, communication, negotiation, conflict resolution, problem solving, goal setting, action planning etc. Do you have all the resources you need to achieve your goals and if no, is there a way to acquire them? It can be helpful to talk to someone you trust about your goals and what you will need to achieve them and get their opinion about further potential resources you may need.

3 The unknown

This is arguably the single most significant barrier to change. When we step out of our 'comfort zone' into an unfamiliar situation with an uncertain outcome, we will experience discomfort. It can take many forms, but the commonest is undoubtedly anxiety: an uncomfortable emotion that we can expect to feel in any challenging situation with an uncertain outcome. If we are not willing to make room for the discomfort of change that accompanies the unknown, we will not engage in activities that are fulfilling but are currently outside of our comfort zone. Remember, actions that align with our values are not always fun, yet they feel satisfyingly fulfilling and enrich the way we spend our time.

Which are your barriers? They can be any of the aforementioned or something else unique to you.

My most common barrier(s) to achieve my goals are:

1 _____

2 _____

3 _____

To overcome those barriers, I will

➢ to come up with concrete and actionable solutions to how you will master the obstacles, think of **who** can help you overcome the barrier, **when** would it be best to address the issue and of course **how** you intend to go about it.

For barrier 1, I will

_____

_____

_____

For barrier 2, I will

_____

_____

_____

For barrier 3, I will

_____

_____

_____

Note

i A new map of wonder by Caspar Henderson.

Bibliography

1 Rogers CR. *On Becoming a Person: A Therapist's View of Psychotherapy*. Robinson; New Ed edition; 2011.
2 Lulé D, Häcker S, Ludolph A, Birbaumer N, Kübler A. Depression and Quality of Life in Patients with Amyotrophic Lateral Sclerosis. *Deutsches Arzteblatt International*. 2008;105(23):397–403. doi:10.3238/arztebl. 2008.0397
3 de Ridder D, Geenen R, Kuijer R, van Middendorp H. Psychological Adjustment to Chronic Disease. *The Lancet*. 2008;372(9634):246–255. doi:10.1016/S0140-6736(08)61078-8
4 Hayes SC, Lillis J. *Acceptance and Commitment Therapy*. American Psychological Association (Theories of Psychotherapy Series); 2012.
5 Markway BG, Ampel C, Flynn T. *The Self-Confidence Workbook: A Guide to Overcoming Self-Doubt and Improving Self-Esteem*. Althea Press; 2018.
6 Shigaki C, Kruse RL, Mehr D, et al. Motivation and Diabetes Self-Management. *Chronic Illness*. 2010;6(3):202–214. doi:10.1177/1742395 310375630
7 Harris R. *The Happiness Trap: Stop Struggling, Start Living*. Robinson Publishing; 2008.
8 Wilson KG, DuFrene T. *Mindfulness for Two: An Acceptance and Commitment Therapy Approach to Mindfulness in Psychotherapy*. New Harbinger Publications; 2009.

Chapter 3

Strengthening body and mind

We all have a philosophical/spiritual beliefs system, and even if we don't articulate them, these philosophical ideas shape the decisions we make. One of these philosophical tenets is our beliefs about the connection between mind and body. The way you think about your condition and approach the symptoms are related to whether you believe the mind and body are separate entities (dualism) or firmly connected (physicalism).

The connection between mind and body has been an interest of philosophers and psychologists for centuries. Descartes, in the 17th century, planted the first seeds of the idea that the body is somewhat connected with the mind. He believed that the mind and body were separate entities, but they could communicate through the nervous system (dualism). In the 20th century, Freud changed our beliefs about the connection of mind and body. Freud believed that physical symptoms could be 'converted' from unconscious emotional conflicts. In other words, the mind can control the body (phenomenalism). Most neuroscientists today reject Freud's theories since for them it's evident that somehow everything that happens in mind must arise from the brain (physicalism).

In the mindfulness courses that I facilitated, the mind-body connection has become the first thing I discuss with people. It's difficult for me to describe what it is that we do in the mindfulness courses. I usually end up talking about training the mind to focus on the present moment and by doing that we gain more control over thoughts and symptoms. Yet, I'm not talking about 'mind over matter', as many of the participants assume.

'Mind over matter' implies that mind and body are different entities and the mind can change physical symptoms. It's a very aspirational idea: we can control what happens in the body with pure will and positive thinking. I'm not saying that the power of the brain cannot change the outcome of the condition, all I'm saying is that to this day we don't have the evidence that such a possibility is real. My stance is somewhat different. First, the body affects the mind; the physiological changes in the body will have an impact on the mind. The effect can be direct – after all the centre of emotions is located in the brain and controlled by hormones – or indirect, through behaviour. What we do will affect how happy or unhappy we will become; for example, there is plenty of evidence on the effects of exercise on improving the mood and alleviating symptoms of depression.[1,2] Second, our emotions have an impact on the body. Depressive symptoms and stress can have a profound effect on how well our immune system works and consequently can exacerbate symptoms. For example, we have scientific evidence for the links between stress and adverse outcome for a wide variety of conditions including chronic heart disease,[3] asthma,[4] autoimmune disease,[5] multiple sclerosis,[6] upper respiratory infection,[7] skin conditions,[8] HIV/AIDS[9] and psoriasis.[10]

Most of us are dualist. Intuitively, we think of mind and body as two different entities. Viewing our body as separate and independent from the mind runs the risk of seeing the bodies as mere vessels, or tools – shells with little value. This can lead to us being less careful with our bodies and more neglectful of our health. In fact, researchers at the University of Cologne, Germany,[11] recently showed that our beliefs on mind and body connection could have an impact on our health. They conducted a series of experiments where volunteers were primed[i] to believe either that mind and body are separate entities or that bodies can directly affect the mind by reading a short text making a case for either. They found out that people who were primed to believe that mind and body are separate entities had a more reckless attitude towards health and exercise; they were less keen to endorse statements such as "I limit the amount of fat I eat" and "I regularly go to the gym" than those primed to believe the body connects with the mind. Asked to pick a cookbook as a reward for participating, people primed to think on the mind-body separation were more likely to choose one on barbecue or desserts over organic and vegetarian ones and they ate less nutritional cafeteria meals when given a choice. Those primed with beliefs about body being the centre of mind were the opposite on all the measures.

Interestingly, it worked the other way around as well. Activating healthy or unhealthy thoughts reinforced the volunteers' philosophies. In other words, when you think about a healthy lifestyle, you are more likely to believe that the mind and body are connected. If you think that mind and body are connected, then you are more likely to think about a healthy lifestyle and behave accordingly.

Therefore, what we believe the connection is between mind and body will affect the way we respond to the symptoms, what we do to maintain a healthy lifestyle and how we proactively plan for future challenges. Let's now look at the evidence that shows the ways the body affects the mind and the mind affects the body.

When the body can help the mind

To a great extent, the brain controls the body. The act of waving your arm, for example, is caused by a particular pattern of neural activity in a certain place in your brain – specifically, the motor cortex in your left frontal lobe. However, research evidence suggests that the brain does not only fully control the body. Our body influences the state of our brain as well.

An example that shows the different pathways of how our body can influence our feelings and thought patterns is the evidence on exercising the body and how this affects our emotions. Studies of how exercise affects depression date back to at least the '80s and more recent evidence supports the effects of exercise on various disease pathogenesis and symptoms. A study published at the *Journal of Affective Disorders* combined the evidence of 23 studies (977 participants) on the effects of exercise on depressive symptoms and showed that physical exercise is an effective intervention for depression and could be a viable adjunct treatment in combination with antidepressants.[12] There is also evidence on the protective effect of regular physical activity on depressive episodes in people with long-term conditions including people with chronic kidney disease[13] and improvements in psychological function and quality of life for people with pain conditions (rheumatoid arthritis, osteoarthritis, fibromyalgia, low back pain, intermittent claudication, dysmenorrhea, mechanical neck disorder, spinal cord injury, post-polio syndrome and patellofemoral pain).[14]

How does exercising the body helps combat depression? There are different ways that the body is linked with the mind. One is that exerting your body muscles causes some minor injuries. Your brain starts to produce endorphins to counteract the painful effects of this. And when you stop exercising the endorphin production drops, but not immediately. For a while – many minutes in some cases – those endorphins continue to be produced and continue to influence the brain. Many people report a feeling of great pleasure when this is happening. The endorphins don't merely dull the physical pain of exercise, but also dull the mental and emotional pain.

Exercise also reduces inflammation via several different processes (inflammation, cytokines, toll-like receptors, adipose tissue and via the vagal tone), which can contribute to better health outcomes for those experiencing mood difficulties.[15]

Not only exercising can make you happier; even forcing a smile will eventually signal to your brain that you are happy, and you will feel happier. German researchers[16] ran a series of experiments where participants hold a pen in their mouth in ways that made them smile or frown. Participants who made the smile posture reported feeling more amused and positive than the participants who adopted that frown posture. You might be familiar with that experiment now, since it has been popularised by the media, but 30 years ago participants had no clue what the real purpose of these experiments was. In fact, the researchers asked people what they thought the experiments were about and none guessed the connection to them feeling happier. That means participants didn't know what the experiment was about as they were participating in it. This basic effect of being made to smile has been replicated many times.

A side note here, this replication is really important. Sometimes you may hear media stories about research studies showing impressive results of some medication or other intervention related to your condition which is promising but you should be tentative in the conclusions that you draw from it. There might be something specific about the population of this one study that does not translate well to the wider population or it might be that the particular group of researchers measured things in certain ways that produce that effect. This is the reason in this book I draw conclusions based on wider literature and I don't rely on single studies when I'm discussing various effects or techniques.

OK, now back to our pencil studies. What was so revolutionary was that they showed that not only our emotions influence the way we act. When we feel happy, we smile, when we are surprised we open our eyes and mouth. But also the information flows in the other direction as well. If the emotional centres of my brain detect that I'm smiling – presumably based on signals coming from the muscles and the brain areas that control them – then they encode that as evidence that I must be happy. If my brain detects that I'm acting happy – then it presumes maybe I am happy.

And smiling doesn't just make you feel happier. It seems to reduce your responses to pain or stress.[17] Smiling boosts immune system function and even boosts the brain's release of serotonin and endorphins. When you find yourself in a stressful situation, you should smile. Making a smile – even a fake smile – will reduce that feeling of stress.

All these studies described here point to a really fascinating idea about the relationship between our brains and the rest of our bodies. Much of modern science has often thought of the brain as a standalone, information-processing device – like the king of the body that makes unilateral calculations and hands down orders to be carried out. The basic idea is that many of the impressive feats that we credit to our cerebrum are actually accomplished by a complex interaction between the brain and the rest of the body. What you do with your body plays an important role in how you feel. That's the reason why when we talk about self-managing a long-term condition, we don't focus on managing only the psychological or only the physical issues but we address things on all fronts to be the most effective self-manager.

How stress enters the body

Alex

Alex was very apprehensive about the effects of stress on his health. He complained that his husband and sons did not understand the detrimental effect of stress on his condition no matter how many times he discussed this with them. His two sons are playing up and keep arguing at the dinner table. His husband is not helping with the household chores. The list goes on. He knows all this stress will harm his condition. He is stressed about being stressed. Which, given the sensational headlines about the detrimental effects of stress is not an uncommon predicament.

Stress is broadly considered an emotional experience and its links to body damages are well known. While it is true that 'stress is bad for your health' as many news reports and magazine articles have warned us, I do want to add the caveat that it is chronic stress that is bad for our health. Stress, in general, is an adaptive biological mechanism that serves a vital role. There are three systems in place that translate stress into body reaction. The central nervous system, the endocrine system and the immune system that organises responses to infections and other challenges.

Humans and other animals have similar biological mechanisms. When there is a threat, the brain will release hormones to activate the immune system; the nervous system that has to do with survival actions (fly or fight) will be in overdrive and the actions that are not that important (rest, digest, reproduce) will be temporarily suspended. When under stress we need these physiological changes to survive.

For short-lived stressors, this is a highly delicate and precise adaptive process, and it is not damaging to the body. Short-lived stressors (5–100 minutes) induce an immune-enhancing effect. A number of studies have also shown that exposure to acute stress may be harnessed to improve immune response to vaccines.[18]

Theo

Theo was attending our online mindfulness course. The sessions were delivered through Skype. Theo wanted to take part in the course despite his fear of technology. The day before the first session, he went to his local technology shop to ask advice about installing and using his video camera. The young employee was patronising, which made Theo feel embarrassed and anxious which made it even harder for him to understand how to use his video camera. Without understanding very well what he needed to do, he purchased a new video camera. He was embarrassed and overwhelmed by the time he arrived at the till which made his Parkinson's disease symptoms more pronounced. He struggled to take money out of his wallet and then put his wallet back in his pocket. People standing behind made him more nervous. The woman at the till smiled and told him not to worry and to take his time, but this made things worse. He felt tears welling up and couldn't leave the shop quickly enough.

All day after the incident at the shop, he felt anxious and embarrassed. The next morning, he called me before the session to check whether the camera worked OK and it did. We chatted about his new camera, and as he was recounting the story at the store, all the emotions came back to him. The effects of the stressful event that could have lasted for less than one hour lasted for the whole day and re-appeared with each retelling of the story.

The stress response is an adaptive and protective mechanism of the body that becomes maladaptive if 'left on' resulting in physiological 'wear and tear'.[19] Stanford Professor Robert Sapolsky[ii] posits that we can turn on the physical stress response with our thoughts, which means that a system designed to be used now ends up being potentially overused when those inevitable hard times come along. As he puts it: "Essentially, we humans live well enough and long enough, and are smart enough, to generate all sorts of stressful events purely in our heads".[20] These events, in turn, wear out our bodies. This is in contrast to animals who tend to use their stress responses for acute physical crises, sometimes for chronic physical challenges, but not so much for psychological and social disruptions.

A rabbit needs to get stressed when chased by a fox. Otherwise, it won't run fast to survive. The stress hormones will send messages to the rabbit's brain that it is under threat so that the immune system is ready to bounce back from any potential injury that might happen during that chase. The rabbit can break a bone while running or maybe the fox manages to bite the rabbit before it escapes, so the immune system chemicals need to float around the body during the chase so they can quickly go to where there is an injury to repair things quickly. The stress signals in the rabbit's brain will also activate the fight or fly nervous system. The heart will start beating faster, blood pressure will increase, breathing will be more rapid, the body might tremble, the muscles will tense up, and all that to help the rabbit run as fast as possible away from the threat and into safety. Also, to reserve energy and resources the brain will shut down the non-essential systems (rest, digestion and reproduction).

Humans' emotions and thoughts are an advantage against animals that are bigger, stronger and faster. Emotions and thoughts help us figure out potential threats and find solutions. However, this mechanism can be a disadvantage when stressors are less physical. As soon as it finds a safe place, the rabbit will go back to enjoying munching roots. For us humans, the physical recovery after experiencing a stressor is delayed as our mind allows the stressor to 'linger on' psychologically. We may feel scared; the fear will generate thoughts, worries about the future and ruminations about the unpleasant experience. And even though the actual threat is not present anymore, having those thoughts will activate the same stress mechanisms for the body.

Further, humans anticipate events, which may elicit stress responses before a stressor. Rabbits will not stress about food when they are fed, but humans may stress about a 20-year mortgage for 20 years. Even though the threat is not real in the sense the human life is not in immediate danger the brain cannot discriminate and will act in the same way.

Chronic activation of the stress systems makes it less likely for the body to return to its pre-stressed state because the stress response itself is altered. In other words, the immune system stops being effective, and that can make us vulnerable to infections and can delay recovery.

Interestingly, when it comes to significant stressors such as grief, divorce or moving house, the body can work through them without too much negative impact on the immune system. However, the daily hassles – the broken computers, the rude receptionist, the parking ticket – can have a more significant and more negative effect on our health. When it comes to major stressful events, such as a bereavement, we put in place the resources and systems available to deal with them. We use social support, we express emotions through creative outlets, and we practice self-kindness. Daily hassles are small, constant and everywhere.

Stress can also enter the body indirectly. When we are stressed we tend to make unhealthy food choices,[21] drink more alcohol and smoke more.[22] We also exercise less[23] and adhere less to treatment regimens.[24] There is also some evidence that patients with type 1 diabetes who experienced daily hassles were more likely to have inadequate glycaemic control.[25]

There is further evidence that chronic stress can increase susceptibility to various conditions and this relationship between stress and disease is independent of traditional risk factors such as smoking, diet, alcohol use or exercise. When we are talking about chronic stressors, we are talking about repeated and prolonged events that linger for months or years with no definite end in sight and are often uncontrollable. For example studies have shown that chronic stressors such as perceived daily stress,[26] caregiving,[27] hostile marital interactions,[28] low socioeconomic status,[29] depression,[30] burnout syndrome/job strain,[31] and post-traumatic disorder[32] are associated with increased in plasma and serum cytokines, which play an essential role in immune response.

Perceptions of stress will activate a series of physiological reactions that aim to boost the immunity of our bodies and prepare them to recover from a physical attack. When the perception of stress is prolonged, this physiological mechanism will remain switched on. This extended activation of the physiological reactions to stress can eventually lead to dysregulation of the stress-response system with negative impact on the immunity system. The key word here is **perceptions** of stress: it doesn't matter whether the stressor is real or imagined, the body will react the same way. And since we cannot do much about the stressors that exist in our environment let's look at what we can do to respond to those stressors and lessen the impact of the perceptions of stress.

Managing negative thoughts and low mood

I am writing this chapter from Greece. I travelled from the UK yesterday. It's the beginning of December, and I left a very grey and cold London. Our flight was early in the morning, and there was hardly any light when I left my house. After two trains and several coffees, I arrived at the airport on time. The sky was dark and ominous, but I was so excited to see my family. We were boarding the plane when it started snowing, and by the time we boarded the snow had covered the runaway and we couldn't leave. We waited on the plane for 4 hours to take off. Nearly 200 people in the aircraft and we all experienced that delay differently. When the announcement was made that we had to wait for a clear runaway, the young guy next to me swore and said that he couldn't believe his bad luck. The person in front opened his laptop and put on his headphones to watch a movie. The woman on the next aisle started a heated argument with the flight attendant, as she demanded free drinks to compensate for the inconvenience of the delay. The lady next to her kept looking at her watch every few minutes, like a ritual that would make the snow disappear.

We were all in the same situation, and we all had a different experience. The person in front of me relaxed watching a movie and munched on the oranges he had brought with him. The person next to me recounted all his bad luck to his friend on the phone. Of course, there were external factors that determined the experience of each of us, such as why we were on that plane and who or what was waiting for us in Greece. But the experience was also determined by three factors that we could control:

1   How well we anticipated problems. As a person with Multiple Sclerosis told me: "I always like to prepare for the worst and hope for the best". Sometimes, if you anticipate things to go the wrong way, when they do, you will not be taken by surprise.

2 How well we planned and prepared in advance. For example, the man in front of me had packed snacks, brought a cosy cardigan with him and had downloaded movies to watch.

3 How flexible we respond to situations. We all have our signature way to react to stress and discomfort. It might be anger, guilt, withdrawal, eating carbs, procrastinate, exercise, talking to friends or getting very organised. Being flexible and having a wider variety of responses takes some practice. Pause for a brief second before you react and review your choices.

There are circumstances beyond our control, and then there are our responses to these circumstances. The circumstances and our responses to them will mould our experience. We can work on and perfect the way we respond to external events, and external events need not play a defining factor in our experience.

When something disrupts what we are expecting or what we are used to, be it a new symptom, an exacerbation, or a particularly stressful day, our brain will generate a lot of unhappy, anxious thoughts. That's fine. This is the brain's job to try to predict worse case scenarios and create solutions.

Tom

> Tom, a 77-year-old man who had been diagnosed with multiple sclerosis for nearly 20 years said to me in one interview, "I used to elevate small problems to major ones and now I realise I can sort of separate the small ones from the large ones". Regular meditation, yoga or tai chi or any of the mind-body rituals can help calm the mind and also can help us to step back from our problems and see them for what they are, so instead of making a mountain out of a molehill, we see their true dimensions.

McKay, Davis and Fanning[33] in their book *Thoughts and Feelings: taking control of your moods and life* talk about 'coping' thoughts. 'Coping' thoughts are one way to answer back to these negative or anxious thoughts and help you manage anxious or depressive responses. Coping statements are truthful, positive statements used to replace the negative thoughts that take over when you feel anxious, stressed, angry and/or when facing other overwhelming situations. For example: replace, "I can't take it anymore" with "I've managed perfectly well in the past, and I can manage again now".

If you want to see what that means in practice, you can start by laying out a map of what is currently happening when you feel stressed and what type of thoughts appear in your mind. Take a moment to think about a stressful situation. See the scene as it unfolds for a couple of minutes and then notice what thoughts come to your mind in this stressful situation. Write those thoughts down. Then you want to start introducing coping ideas. The key questions to ask yourself when coming up with coping thoughts are:

- Do I have a plan to handle this situation?
- What would I do if the thing I fear took place?
- How likely are the scary outcomes that I imagine?
- Can I estimate the odds against these are happening?
- How long would I have to bear this if I were really in this situation? – Sometimes it's enough to remind yourself, "I can do this; it's only a short time".
- What coping skills do I have to handle this?
- How can I relax?

Negative mood is not a permanent state and through monitoring with modification, we can often change the types of thoughts we have about the situations we face. Through awareness, we can monitor automatic negative thoughts and seek ways to modify them into positive thoughts, in the end replacing negative mood with a more positive, happy mood. Learning how to experience even the smallest amount of pleasure in our lives is key to lifting negative mood. Not being able to find pleasure may result from taking part in activities that were not pleasurable even before you felt bad. Also, in negative mood, negative thoughts are stronger than any other thoughts. When our thoughts are negative, we are not able to find pleasure in pleasant activities.

The other way to deal with these negative thoughts is to acknowledge them and let them be, so they are present but we do not engage with them. For example, sitting in the delayed airplane you might be getting stressed about potentially missing your pre-booked train. Acknowledge that those thoughts are present, while you switch your attention to your newspaper and the crossword you were working on earlier. To take this one step further, limit your expectations. And by that I don't mean to lower but to banish them. Yes, that's right. If and whenever you can, avoid expecting anything good or bad to happen. This will avert – to a certain extent – the generation of negative and stressful thoughts. This more accepting and less intervening way of dealing with thoughts became very popular with the publication of Kabat-Zinn's book[34] *Full Catastrophe living: how to cope with stress, pain and illness using mindfulness meditation.* Jon Kabat-Zinn, who popularised mindfulness meditation in the West, professes that having no expectations at all, good or bad, will lead to a 'beginner's mind' where the mind will be more alert, open and present at the moment. If we expect something good to happen and it doesn't happen, we will be upset and disappointed. If we expect something wrong to happen, we will get anxious regardless of whether it does or does not occur.

Whatever works better for you. Change negative thoughts with 'coping' ones or if you prefer let thoughts be without too much interference. Either way, it doesn't make much difference in the outcome. The critical point of both these approaches is the ability to see our experiences differently. We need to change the way we relate to our thoughts to respond differently to the situations we face. The aim is to see our thoughts as something we can observe, and we have the choice to control or not. If it feels more natural to see things positively, go ahead and look at the bright side of things. If you find it difficult to reframe things that annoy you, try to remind yourself that these are just thoughts, you and no one else can predict the future.

Another way to respond to feeling low is to alter what you do. Simply put, to feel happier, you need to add activities in your life that will make you happier. Living well with a long-term health condition is not only about staying on top of various symptoms and challenges. It is also about adding into your life fun activities, things that you enjoy. Even the smallest bit of satisfaction can result in optimism if we give credit to our own actions for causing it. If we practice having good feelings and being aware of them, we strengthen our ability to feel more good things in our lives. Pleasant activities include having a warm or cool drink, going for a walk, or calling someone you care about.

We can also focus on activities that offer us a sense of mastery. Mastery involves a judgment of how well we did something based on how difficult it is for us just the way we are right now, not how we might ideally be some day. Mastery, or skill, occurs when we pay attention to what we were able to get done and not what we didn't get done. Do things that you value, things that you are good at and they give you a sense of achievement. Achievement activities include clearing out a drawer, paying a bill, or doing some work in the garden like pulling some weeds or trimming a bush.

There is a difference between pleasure and mastery. Some activities offer us one or the other, or they can offer us both, together. Whatever you do, focus your full attention on what you are doing.

Besides finding ways to include pleasure or mastery activities in every day, it is also important to develop or strengthen our ability to be aware of the experiences as fully as possible. This can include becoming aware of how the body felt during the experiences, what mood or thoughts were present during the experiences, and what we thought of the experiences after they were over. Awareness allows us to experience and appreciate more fully; awareness helps us notice what even slightly positive things may be occurring in our daily lives, and brings our attention to the thoughts, feelings, and/or bodily sensations that accompany pleasant experiences.

To summarise, when we experience negative thoughts or low mood, there are a few things we can do. We can identify the negative thoughts that tend to pop in our mind more frequently and find coping thoughts to replace them as a conscious response. We can also try not to feed the negative thoughts' narrative. Don't feed the negative thoughts; prevent them from escalating. We can also add in our days activities that are fun or let us feel that we achieved something.

Coping with stress

With the effort required to get by each day, you can forget to reflect on how you live each day. Did you act with intention and according to your plans and values or merely react to whatever happened to you in a mechanic fashion? Did your choices reflect your needs and dreams, or did you choose a path as a reaction to stressful events?

Sam

Sam was a TV production manager. For his work, he had different responsibilities, from working out budgets to sorting out staffing for TV programmes. He loved his job and the fast pace of the industry, always on the go. He worked with the same small team for the past 11 years; they were like family to him. Every new contract or job was an uplifting event, approached with great care and interest. After being diagnosed with Parkinson's disease, he was determined not to tell anyone and carry on as usual. He spent hours agonising over logistics of how to accomplish certain things without anyone noticing his difficulties with speech or his walking. But as the condition progressed, it was more and more difficult to disguise it. He said job stress coupled with the weight of keeping his condition concealed harmed his health. So, he quit his job.

His mother was housebound and needed help, and since his brother was living closer, had assumed the majority of the caring. This arrangement was a constant source of dispute with both his mother and brother that also stressed him a lot. After quitting his job, he started minimising contact with his brother, and mother.

Sam was trying to eliminate stressors in his life. He spent a lot of time alone at home and even though this was the opposite of what he used to enjoy he wanted to be OK with it now.

Forcing enjoyment when there is none is hard. Eliminating things from your life without any replacements can deprive you of the rich texture of life. Trying to minimise the stressors can in cases be futile. Life provides us with stress without asking. There will be rude people, broken computers, mixed-up dates of medical appointments, traffic and leaking water pipes. Also, there is the 'positive stress' that you don't want to miss out on, the stress that accompanies happy and essential changes, such as meeting new people, going to social functions, taking up new hobbies, initiating difficult but necessary discussions with loved ones.

Write down your current stressors. Some of them are illness-related, such as pain or fatigue, dealing with a range of healthcare staff, hospital environment and treatments. Others are emotional or social, such as preserving emotional balance, self-image and sense of mastery and control, sustaining existing relationships and managing uncertainty.

Then, score each stressor on a scale 1 to 5 on how much control you feel you have over them. For example, you might feel more in control when you are moving to a new house because there are tangible things you can do to address this stressor. You can ask people for advice on different locations, you can sign up with a few estate agencies to send you information about houses that are available to rent and you can ask an occupational therapist about home modifications. You can score this stressor as maybe a 4 out of 10. On the other hand, the uncertainty of the prognosis of your condition is stressful, but not much can be done. You can read about it on relevant and reliable websites, you can ask your doctor for more information so that you know what the likely progression or treatments scenarios are, but you won't be able to tell for sure how your condition will develop. So, you might score this stressor as a 2 out of 10.

Once you have identified the challenges and how much control you have over them, you can start thinking about the strategies to manage those challenges. 'Emotion-focused' strategies are more helpful for demands we don't have much power over. These help you manage your emotions around the challenge. Such strategies might include writing a diary about what is happening and how you feel about things, talking to friends over drinks about what worries you, taking a yoga or meditation class to help quiet the mind or even taking up a creative hobby to help you express your emotions through art.

For the stressors that you do have more control over, 'problem-focused' strategies might be the best way forward; taking baby steps to resolve the issue actively. Take cognitive fog, for example, a symptom of many conditions, which manifests as difficulty concentrating, paying attention and working through problems. Often it prevents you from completing work tasks on time and to the standards you want them. To solve this issue, you can ask your employer to give you the most important tasks early on in the day, and not surprise you with new demands at 3 p.m. You can delegate some of the tasks that are not the core of your job to other colleagues. This will not only reduce your workload, but also teach you a valuable skill – appropriately delegating tasks to the right people, giving them specific instructions and following up progress. Other things you can do is to say 'no' to jobs that are not relevant to what you have been employed to do. In other words, cut down any 'volunteer work' you do for your employer and stick to the tasks that are required of you.

Finally, write down your metric of success. How will you know that you have addressed the problem sufficiently? A measure of success might be that your to-do list is no longer than five items each day, or that you no longer feel completely wiped out at the end of the day.

Challenges	Control Level 1 (not much)– 5 (complete control)	Best way to cope	Success metric
e.g. illness progression	2	Talk to my health care team about my worries. Every time I feel panicky about the future, take some time to focus on breathing; if I can't concentrate on breathing, put on some music and pay attention to the music	I don't think about the illness progression three evenings of the week.

Instead of (or in addition to) avoiding stress, you can find ways to manage it. There is a wide variety of useful stress management techniques. A great way to relax is using a technique called progressive muscle relaxation.

Progressive muscle relaxation is an exercise that relaxes your mind and body by progressively tensing and relaxing muscle groups throughout your entire body. Begin by finding a comfortable position either sitting or lying down in a location where you will not be interrupted. Allow your attention to focus only on your body. If you begin to notice your mind wandering, bring it back to the muscle you are working on. Take a deep breath through your abdomen, hold for a few seconds, and exhale slowly. Again, as you breathe notice your stomach rising and your lungs filling with air. As you exhale, imagine the tension in your body being released and flowing out of your body. The idea of the progressive muscle relaxation technique is that you tense each muscle group vigorously, but without straining, and then release the tension and feel the muscle relax. You tense each muscle for about 5 seconds. If you have any pain or discomfort at any of the targeted muscle groups omit that step. It is important that you keep breathing throughout the exercise. You start by tightening the muscles in your forehead by raising your eyebrows as high as you can. Hold for about 5 seconds. Then release, feeling that tension fall away. Pause for about 10 seconds. Now smile widely, feeling your mouth and cheeks tense. Hold for about 5 seconds, then release, appreciating the softness in your face. Pause for about 10 seconds. Next, tighten your eye muscles by squinting your eyelids tightly shut. Hold for about 5 seconds, and release. Pause for about 10 seconds. Gently pull your head back as if to look at the ceiling. Hold for about 5 seconds, and release, feeling the tension melting away. Pause for about 10 seconds. Now feel the weight of your relaxed head and neck sink. Now, tightly, but without straining, clench your fists and hold this position for about 5 seconds, and release. Pause for about 10 seconds. Now, flex your biceps. Hold for about 5 seconds, and release. Now tighten your triceps by extending your arms out and locking your elbows. Hold for about 5 seconds, and release. Pause for about 10 seconds. Now lift your shoulders up as if they could touch your ears. Hold for about 5 seconds, and quickly release, feeling their heaviness. Pause for about 10 seconds. Tense your upper back by pulling your shoulders back trying to make your shoulder blades touch. Hold for about 5 seconds, and release. Pause for about 10 seconds. Tighten your chest by taking a deep breath in, hold for about 5 seconds, and exhale, blowing out all the tension. Now tighten the muscles in your stomach by sucking in. Hold for about 5 seconds, and release. Pause for about 10 seconds. Gently arch your lower back. Hold for about 5 seconds, relax. Pause for about 10 seconds. Tighten your buttocks. Hold for about 5 seconds and release. Pause for about 10 seconds. Tighten your thighs by pressing your knees together, as if you were holding a penny between them. Hold for about 5 seconds and release. Pause for about 10 seconds. Now flex your feet, pulling your toes towards you and feeling the tension in your calves. Hold for about 5 seconds, and relax, feel the weight of your legs sinking down. Pause for about 10 seconds. Curl your toes under, tensing your feet. Hold for about 5 seconds, release. Pause for about 10 seconds. Finally, imagine a wave of relaxation slowly spreading through your body beginning at your head and going all the way down to your feet.

Doing yoga, tai chi or meditation can also help with feeling more relaxed and help you respond to stress more effectively. You can search for yoga classes that focus on long-term conditions or generic ones. If you live in a big city, it's very likely there will be meditation centres that you can join but also the internet is full of free meditation practices that you can try.

Another way that can help you feel in control is to approach stressful situations differently. When presented with a problem, stretch your imagination to find new and innovative solutions. Before giving up or opting for half-measures, try to think of alternatives. As with every skill the more you practice the better you become at it; you can also get more ideas if you talk to others or observe them to see how they find solutions to issues. Finally, another way to sharpen your problem-solving skills is to learn more about your problem, or your condition. More information usually gives us more ideas.

Planning and managing your time efficiently can also reduce unnecessary stress. For example, having to buy a present for someone if left for the last minute can be a stressful experience but it can be a pleasant activity if you are out in the shops early enough to give yourself time to browse and choose thoroughly. Use any tools that appeal to you. Notebooks, post-it notes, Excel spreadsheets, mobile phone apps, anything that can help you plan what needs to be done and when and to help you remember the plans you made. Being prepared can save you from a lot of unnecessary stress.

Another way to reduce stress or handle it better is to discuss your intention to better manage stress openly and respectfully. Express your needs and ask for what you want. Try to avoid the trap of accusations and opt to start with 'I' statements followed by the way you feel followed by the reason you feel this way. "I feel ignored when you look at your phone when we're having dinner" rather than "You always ignore me". This invites open communication. People are less likely to get defensive or argue with how you feel. You feel how you feel, and you model a way for them also to express their feelings. See more details on communication skills in Chapter 7.

Other people can be a great source of comfort, and different people can help in various ways that add value. Having someone understand what you are going through and offer love and trust is invaluable and can help you see the situation from different perspectives. People can also provide tangible support and help you sort out issues that cause you stress. Friends, family and acquaintances can also help by giving advice, suggestions and information. They can make you aware of things you wouldn't have even thought to ask or to search for yourself. Finally, others can also give you feedback in certain situations and review with you what went wrong and how to fix things. Read also Chapter 7 for ideas to improve your communication and deepen your relationships.

Pearl

Pearl did not have a comfortable life by most people's standards. She had lost her father when she was a teenager. Her mum was battling cancer for the past ten years. She had juvenile idiopathic arthritis, and recently she had two painful and complicated surgeries. But you couldn't tell she was going through all this hardship. Pearl loved to participate in research studies; she was learning things and also her contribution could help others in the future. She also loved going to the gym. She had a personal trainer and had loved trialling different types of yoga. She liked traveling and she's been to a few places around Europe with her girlfriends the past year. One year, she decided to dye her hair blue to raise money for a charity. Nothing indicates she is in a lot of physical pain. She thinks the secret is to have a lot of people in your life. Her family and friends are fantastic, and they are very close. She has people who come around with food when they know she had a rough day, friends are taking turns coming to medical appointments with her, she can talk to her mum when she gets upset but most importantly spending time with her friends and family is great fun for her. She doesn't talk much about her conditions and how badly the symptoms affect her. She's interested in her friends' lives. What they are up to. They always come to her for advice. But when she needs something she knows she can ask them and they will offer all the help they can.

Pearl was very proactive with her social life. She loved being with people and being with people was the best way for her to deal with stresses in her life. Taking care of her body by regularly exercising, eating healthily and practising meditation was a priority for her. She built all the support and coping strategies and when she hit a rough patch with her condition, she had the cushioning she needed to protect her from stress and anxiety.

It is important to be flexible with your stress management techniques. We all have our favourite go-to strategies. Having a long-term condition will require you to consider new strategies as the condition or circumstances change. That is why it is helpful from time to time to review the ways you've chosen to manage stress.

Future planning to feel good in mind and body

We try to anticipate future circumstances and their impact on ourselves and close others. We take these expected future consequences and our personal goals and values into account when deciding on what to do next. We also must balance long- versus short-term interests in cases where actions may serve one goal at the expense of another. Research has shown that proactively preparing for barriers to self-management of a long-term condition is a successful strategy in maintaining new behaviours.[35]

Forethought can keep stress under control by building resources in advance. With future planning you translate an abstract long-term concern into more concrete achievable goal you can deal with in the present. Thinking about goals in advance may help you become aware of other competing goals, habits and activities that may undermine your motivation to recognise your limited resources. Future thinking and planning also will give you time to think about things that could go wrong and plan alternative strategies to deal with problem situations as they arise.

But you need to use your judgement, so you don't spend a lot of your current resources for a very unlikely future issue. The future planning needs to be effective so that it doesn't exacerbate the problem. Research has also shown that being in a positive mood can make you better in future planning by increasing your ability to identify what you need to achieve your goal and increasing the enjoyment you feel when doing dull-but-required tasks as well as fun and interesting tasks.

It is a good idea to start planning and preparing for future potential challenges, to be fully prepared when they come or even prevent them. It's an act of taking best care of ourselves before problems arise. So, how can we gather the best possible resources to help our future selves? Let's start from the basics: are we taking care of our bodies the best possible way? Eating a healthy balanced diet, doing some form of exercising, not smoking, not drinking excessively, retaining a correct posture when sitting or standing? The healthier you are, the easier it would be to fight off stress both mentally and physically, engaging in an appropriate type of physical exercise at a proper level. I will discuss more how to make these changes and stick with them in Chapter 6.

Next we can move to a second stage of gathering resources. Other people can be an extremely valuable asset for potential future challenges to help us both emotionally and practically. Do we maintain the relationships with significant others? Do we communicate with them regularly? Do we create memories and moments together? Are we available to help and support them when they need our help? And what about new friends? Are we open to meet new people? Take up hobbies where we can meet like-minded people? Hang out at book readings, and movie openings, galleries, illness-related talks and seminars, and be prepared to chat and connect with others? See also Chapter 7 for more ideas on how to deepen your relationships and improve communication.

Maria

Maria is a master of planning and positivity. She thinks through all potential challenges and plans meticulously for the future to make sure she can cope with all worse case scenarios whether or not they materialise. The first course of action for Maria is always to gather as much information as she can to understand what is happening and what is likely to happen. Meticulous planning for all eventualities was a part of her job and being prepared gives her a sense of control over unpredictable conditions.

Given the uncertainty of her Multiple Sclerosis prognosis, planning things in case her condition worsens gives her something concrete to do. For example, she was looking into house modifications to make her kitchen more functional; cleaners to come once a week; she experimented with 'pick and drop' laundry services; and at some point, she looked into hiring a cook to help her prepare meals for the week and put away in the freezer for her and her family. For her everything is about goal setting, planning, expecting challenges and coming up with solutions.

She has learned to ask for help when needed. It was hard to do in the beginning as she was very independent and liked to do things on her own, but she started seeing the positives of asking for help. She was able to make a lot of connections with people that she would otherwise have ignored because she had to stop and ask for help. Getting tangible and emotional support from her family and friends also helped her manage stress now and in the future.

Finally, make a coping plan for when challenges arise. Write down things that stress you and potential ways to manage them.

For example:

Stressor	Solution
e.g. getting on and off the train	One stop before I need to leave the train, I'll make sure I gather my belongings, put them in my bag, find my ticket and put it somewhere that is easily accessible, put my coat, hat and gloves on, so as soon as the train arrives to my stop I'm ready to hop off.

An important way to better manage future stressors or prevent them is to keep things light and fun. Create a list of activities that you enjoy and activities that give you a sense of satisfaction. Ask yourself, what do I need for myself right now? How can I best take care of myself right now? Even if you don't feel like doing anything, select at least one activity and do it anyway.

It could be visiting or calling friends and family, going for a walk, seeing a movie or a show, listening to or making music, dancing around the room, relaxing with your favourite hot drink, watching something uplifting on TV, reading something pleasurable, making a craft, painting or writing, having a warm bath, getting a massage, sitting in a peaceful place, eating a delicious treat or maybe having a picnic. Or you could do something that will give you a sense of accomplishment like doing your physio exercises, making a healthy meal, doing some gardening, cleaning out a drawer or a closet, repairing something, helping a child with homework, paying your bills, planning lunch boxes for the following days of the week, decorating your house, returning a phone call, writing in a journal, washing the dishes, going shopping or doing something that you have been putting it off.[33] And remember while you are involved in any of those activities to act mindfully, pay full attention to the activity you are doing, break the big tasks into smaller steps (e.g. just do 10 minutes of it). To make sure you have pleasurable activities or activities that make you feel a sense of achievement within your days and weeks, make sure you schedule these activities into your days in advance. Make them part of your weekly schedule.

Then, before you do any of the activities on your list, make another list of the rewards you will get for each activity that you do. Be sure that you follow through and give yourself the reward for each activity that you do. Nothing beats some positive reinforcement.

Combining the techniques discussed in this chapter can yield the best results. Let's say you are stressing about a forthcoming airplane journey, lying awake at night wondering what you are going to do if you need the loo on the plane or how you would cope with the fatigue you are bound to feel in a 12-hour flight etc. Try to replace any unhelpful thoughts with more helpful; "There is no way I can travel on a plane for so long on my own" could become a less threatening one like "It may be challenging, but a lot of people in my circumstances have done it, and it was OK". With planning and forethought, you could prepare well ahead of the journey by searching online for travel tips and contacting specialised travel agencies. Finally, you could reduce your feelings of anxiety by regularly practising deep breathing.

Notes

i Priming is a technique in psychology used to train a person's memory subconsciously. For example, a person who sees the word 'yellow' will be slightly faster to recognise the word 'banana'. This happens because yellow and banana are closely linked in memory.

ii Professor Sapolsky is a very knowledgeable and engaging neuroscientist; I highly recommend watching some of his lectures on depression, stress and human behaviour.

Bibliography

1 Bernstein EE, McNally RJ. Examining the Effects of Exercise on Pattern Separation and the Moderating Effects of Mood Symptoms. *Behavior Therapy.* 2019;50(3):582–593. doi:10.1016/j.beth.2018.09.007

2 Szuhany KL, Bugatti M, Otto MW. A Meta-Analytic Review of the Effects of Exercise on Brain-Derived Neurotrophic Factor. *Journal of Psychiatric Research.* 2015;60:56–64. doi:10.1016/j.jpsychires.2014. 10.003

3 Wirtz PH, von Känel R. Psychological Stress, Inflammation, and Coronary Heart Disease. *Current Cardiology Reports.* 2017;19(11). doi:10. 1007/s11886-017-0919-x

4 Lu Y, Ng TP, Larbi A. Psychological Stress and Asthma: A Mini-Review of the Neuroendocrine-Immune Responses and the Mediation of Neuropeptide Y. *Proceedings of the Nature Research Society.* 2018;2. doi:10.11605/j.pnrs.201802005

5 Song H, Fang F, Tomasson G, et al. Association of Stress-Related Disorders with Subsequent Autoimmune Disease. *JAMA: Journal of the American Medical Association.* 2018;319(23):2388–2400. doi:10. 1001/jama.2018.7028

6 Mitsonis CI, Potagas C, Zervas I, Sfagos K. The Effects of Stressful Life Events on the Course of Multiple Sclerosis: A Review. *International Journal of Neuroscience.* 2009;119(3):315–335. doi:10.1080/00207 450802480192

7 Cohen S. Psychological Stress and Susceptibility to Upper Respiratory Infections. *American Journal of Respiratory and Critical Care Medicine.* 1995;152(4 Pt 2):S53–S58. doi:10.1164/ajrccm/152.4_Pt_2.S53

8 Orion E, Wolf R. Psychological Factors in Skin Diseases: Stress and Skin: Facts and Controversies. *Clinics in Dermatology.* 2013;31(6):707–711. doi:10.1016/j.clindermatol.2013.05.006

9 Leserman J. Role of Depression, Stress, and Trauma in HIV Disease Progression. *Psychosomatic Medicine.* 2008;70(5):539–545. doi:10. 1097/PSY.0b013e3181777a5f

10 Tampa M, Sarbu MI, Mitran MI, Mitran CI, Matei C, Georgescu SR. The Pathophysiological Mechanisms and the Quest for Biomarkers in Psoriasis, a Stress-Related Skin Disease. *Disease Markers.* 2018;2018. doi:10.1155/2018/5823684

11 Forstmann M, Burgmer P, Mussweiler T. "The Mind Is Willing, But the Flesh Is Weak": The Effects of Mind-Body Dualism on Health Behavior. *Psychological Science.* 2012;23(10):1239–1245. doi:10.1177/ 0956797612442392

12 Kvam S, Kleppe CL, Nordhus IH, Hovland A. Exercise as a Treatment for Depression: A Meta-Analysis. *Journal of Affective Disorders.* 2016;202:67–86. doi:10.1016/j.jad.2016.03.063

13 Zhu F-X, Zhang X-Y, Ding X-K, Han B. Protective Effect of Regular Physical Activity on Major Depressive Episodes in Patients with Early

Stages of Chronic Kidney Disease. *Renal Failure*. 2017;39(1):602–606. doi:10.1080/0886022X.2017.1361833

14 Geneen LJ, Moore RA, Clarke C, Martin D, Colvin LA, Smith BH. Physical Activity and Exercise for Chronic Pain in Adults: An Overview of Cochrane Reviews. *Cochrane Database of Systematic Reviews*. 2017;2017(4). doi:10.1002/14651858.CD011279.pub3

15 Mikkelsen K, Stojanovska L, Polenakovic M, Bosevski M, Apostolopoulos V. Exercise and Mental Health. *Maturitas*. 2017;106:48–56. doi:10.1016/j.maturitas.2017.09.003

16 Strack F, Martin LL, Stepper S. Inhibiting and Facilitating Conditions of the Human Smile: A Nonobtrusive Test of the Facial Feedback Hypothesis. *Journal of Personality and Social Psychology*. 1988;54(5):768–777. doi:10.1037/0022-3514.54.5.768

17 Kraft TL, Pressman SD. Grin and Bear It: The Influence of Manipulated Facial Expression on the Stress Response. *Psychological Science*. 2012;23(11):1372–1378. doi:10.1177/0956797612445312

18 Pascoe AR, Fiatarone Singh MA, Edwards KM. The Effects of Exercise on Vaccination Responses: A Review of Chronic and Acute Exercise Interventions in Humans. *Brain, Behavior, and Immunity*. 2014;39:33–41. doi:10.1016/j.bbi.2013.10.003

19 McEwen BS. Stress, Adaptation, and Disease: Allostasis and Allostatic Load. *Annals of the New York Academy of Sciences*. 1998;840(1):33–44. doi:10.1111/j.1749-6632.1998.tb09546.x

20 Sapolsky RM. *Why Zebras Don't Get Ulcers*. Manhattan, NY: Times Books; 2004.

21 O'Connor DB, Jones F, Conner M, McMillan B, Ferguson E. Effects of Daily Hassles and Eating Style on Eating Behavior. *Health Psychology*. 2008;27(1 Suppl.). doi:10.1037/0278-6133.27.1.S20

22 Steptoe A, Wardle J, Pollard TM, Canaan L, Davies GJ. Stress, Social Support and Health-Related Behavior: A Study of Smoking, Alcohol Consumption and Physical Exercise. *Journal of Psychosomatic Research*. 1996;41(2):171–180. doi:10.1016/0022-3999(96)00095-5

23 Ng DM, Jeffery RW. Relationships between Perceived Stress and Health Behaviors in a Sample of Working Adults. *Health Psychology*. 2003;22(6):638–642. doi:10.1037/0278-6133.22.6.638

24 Roohafza H, Kabir A, Sadeghi M, et al. Stress as a Risk Factor for Noncompliance with Treatment Regimens in Patients with Diabetes and Hypertension. *ARYA Atherosclerosis*. 2016;12(4):166–171. doi:10.22122/arya.v12i4.1297

25 Riazi A, Pickup J, Bradley C. Daily Stress and Glycaemic Control in Type 1 Diabetes: Individual Differences in Magnitude, Direction, and Timing of Stress-Reactivity. *Diabetes Research and Clinical Practice*. 2004;66(3):237–244. doi:10.1016/j.diabres.2004.04.001

26 Goldman N, Glei DA, Seplaki C, Liu IW, Weinstein M. Perceived Stress and Physiological Dysregulation in Older Adults. *Stress*. 2005;8(2):95–105. doi:10.1080/10253890500141905

27 Kiecolt-Glaser JK, Preacher KJ, MacCallum RC, Atkinson C, Malarkey WB, Glaser R. Chronic Stress and Age-Related Increases in the Proinflammatory Cytokine IL-6. *Proceedings of the National Academy of Sciences of the United States of America*. 2003;100(15):9090–9095. doi:10.1073/pnas.1531903100

28 Kiecolt-Glaser JK, Loving TJ, Stowell JR, et al. Hostile Marital Interactions, Proinflammatory Cytokine Production, and Wound Healing. *Archives of General Psychiatry*. 2005;62(12):1377–1384. doi:10.1001/archpsyc.62.12.1377

29 Steptoe A, Owen N, Kunz-Ebrecht S, Mohamed-Ali V. Inflammatory Cytokines, Socioeconomic Status, and Acute Stress Responsivity. *Brain, Behavior, and Immunity*. 2002;16(6):774–784. doi:10.1016/S0889-1591(02)00030-2

30 Raison CL, Capuron L, Miller AH. Cytokines Sing the Blues: Inflammation and the Pathogenesis of Depression. *Trends in Immunology*. 2006;27(1):24–31. doi:10.1016/j.it.2005.11.006

31 Grossi G, Perski A, Evengård B, Blomkvist V, Orth-Gomér K. Physiological Correlates of Burnout Among Women. *Journal of Psychosomatic Research*. 2003;55(4):309–316. doi:10.1016/s0022-3999(02)00633-5

32 von Känel R, Hepp U, Kraemer B, et al. Evidence for Low-Grade Systemic Proinflammatory Activity in Patients with Posttraumatic Stress Disorder. *Journal of Psychiatric Research*. 2007;41(9):744–752. doi:10.1016/j.jpsychires.2006.06.009

33 McKay M, Davis M, Fanning P. *Thoughts & Feelings: Taking Control of Your Moods & Your Life*. Oakland, CA: New Harbinger Publications; 2011.

34 Kabat-Zinn J. *Full Catastrophe Living: How to Cope with Stress, Pain and Illness Using Mindfulness Meditation*. Piatkus; 2013.

35 Thoolen BJ, de Ridder D, Bensing J, Gorter K, Rutten G. Beyond Good Intentions: The Role of Proactive Coping in Achieving Sustained Behavioural Change in the Context of Diabetes Management. *Psychology & Health*. 2009;24(3):237–254. doi:10.1080/08870440701864504

Chapter 4

Symptoms management

I attended a round table where people with a long-term condition, researchers and clinicians came together to discuss what it means to 'manage' a long-term condition and even whether the term 'manage' is an appropriate one. The people with the long-term conditions said they would not necessarily use the term. They don't 'manage' their life, they just live their life, and similarly, they live with the condition and do what is necessary to carry on. Researchers, on the other hand, dissect the term and talk about all the different tasks you have to undertake to live harmoniously with the condition. The tasks are multi-levelled and complex.

Frequently, when I interview or work with people with a long-term condition, I get the impression that they underestimate and undervalue what it takes to live with a long-term condition. People will talk about the negative and positive impact of the illness on their lives. They have reflected on how the illness has changed things for them, but they will have difficulty describing how they manage their condition. One reason for that might well be that people don't actually understand what I'm after and another can be that they haven't thought about their condition in these terms. Some people may say "I can't do anything to make things better, it's beyond my control"; others will list the medication they're taking and the medical appointments they are attending. But things are much more complicated. When you have a long-term condition, you are bound to perform tasks that require various skills and manage precise balances without even realising it.

Think about what you have to do each day. Maybe you cooked a nutritious meal, you tightened the loose handle in your bathroom, you followed up with your GP about a referral, you booked taxis for your next hospital appointment, you woke up early to do your physiotherapy exercises, you created a list of what you'd like your carer to do for the day, you looked into buying a second-hand automatic car that won't break the bank. I could carry on with the examples forever, but I'll stop here. You get the idea. If you break down the tasks you perform, you will realise the skills required to accomplish them. You plan, you organise, you execute, you delegate, you supervise. You possess some of those skills already, and you are developing new ones.

In the second chapter, I talked about how following your values gives meaning to your life. In this chapter, we'll explore how managing the long-term condition contributes to the quality of life.

First, you need to acknowledge the various and complex tasks you are ticking off, day in and day out. Second, you need to value the importance of those tasks. You wouldn't trust anyone else to make the final decisions on how to run things. You might get some help, for example, to shift through recommendations of osteopaths and chiropractors but you are the one who will make the final decision of who is the most appropriate practitioner for you to visit. Taking a more proactive role managing your condition will not only make you feel more in charge and give you some control back but also ultimately makes you glide through your day smoothly, elevate your every day and reduce avoidable stress.

For me, symptom management means staying on top of what is required to keep symptoms under control so that they don't rule your life and at the same time live your best life.

Managing pain

Seven point eight million people live with chronic pain. Pain is a common symptom shared among many people with long-term conditions. Pain can come from inflammation, damage in or around joints and tissues, insufficient blood supply to muscles or organs, irritated nerves and other sources. When something hurts, the muscles in that area become tense. This is your body's natural reaction to pain when trying to protect the damaged area. In addition, stress can also make you tense your muscles. These tense muscles can cause soreness or pain.

It won't come as a surprise to you that the pain is closely related to other symptoms, mobility limitations, depression, anxiety and sleep disturbances. Consequently, these other symptoms can lead to avoidance behaviour, unhelpful thoughts and beliefs and emotional difficulties. In turn, these behaviours, thoughts and emotions can lead back to increased pain. For example, pain keeps you awake at night, and because you can't sleep, you keep looking at the clock, thinking that with this restless night you won't be able to function properly the next day and you start feeling anxious which makes it even more unlikely that you will fall asleep by being so worked up and then poor sleep by itself or in combination with all the other thoughts, emotions and behaviour patterns can make pain worse. Stress, anxiety and emotions such as depression, anger, fear and frustration are all normal responses to living with a long-term condition and they can increase your pain and discomfort. When you are stressed, angry, afraid, or depressed, everything, including your pain, seems worse.

What does it mean to manage your pain? Surely the point must be to rid yourself of the pain and not 'manage' it. A lot of people with a long-term condition have 'managing pain' high on their agenda. Living with unending pain can play havoc with any plans of spending your time meaningfully and with intention. Although eliminating the pain might not be feasible for a lot of people, finding ways to gain some control over the pain so it is less overwhelming might be a more realistic goal.

Research evidence demonstrates that there isn't much correlation between changes in pain and other psychological outcome[1,2] and numerous studies have shown that very good treatment outcomes can be achieved without pain reduction.[3,4,5] If pain cannot effectively be reduced, the content of the thoughts and beliefs about pain appears to be a good place to start working.

With thoughts, we can create situations as if they are actually present even though we have never experience them directly. If you want to set up your own business or travel the world, the mind is a great tool, but if you want, for example, to feel happy all the time, to face uncertainty without anxiety, or stop feeling intractable pain, it is an unreliable tool. Your beliefs about your pain, your situation, yourself, your coping resources and the healthcare system affect your reports of pain, but they also are associated with levels of activity, disability and response to treatment. In turn, becoming less active can lead to a weakening of the muscles, or muscle deconditioning. When a muscle becomes weak, it tends to complain whenever it is used. This is why even the slightest activity can sometimes lead to pain and stiffness. On the other hand, you may be determined to prove that you can still be active, so you over-exert yourself. This increases the pain and leads to more inactivity, more depression and yet more pain. Avoiding activities because of the pain can ultimately lead to more pain. The way we can combat this naturally occurring avoidance when it comes to pain is by accepting that pain is part of your condition. Avoiding activities can lead to disuse, disability and depression that can exacerbate the pain.[6,7] We humans are active problem-solving agents. The misdirected problem-solving drive can sometimes be a mission impossible, an insoluble problem. On the other hand, you might want to carry on everything you used to do despite being in pain. You have some ideas of how things should be and you want to get back to what you consider your normal life disregarding any signals from your body. In some case though, this perseverance can lead to frustration, distress, hypervigilance and further disability.

The toughest challenge when it comes to managing your pain and most of the symptoms is to battle your own mind. It's true your mind loves you and will never hurt you but also your mind wants to take short cuts and worries far too much about the future. So, how do you win against your mind? Simply by recognising its tricks, acknowledging that they are only tricks and letting them go.

You might have thoughts like "If I wake up feeling pain my day is ruined", or "If I ask my colleagues to reschedule the meeting, they'll think I'm not pulling my weight" or "Nothing has worked to help me with the pain, so these techniques won't help either". These thoughts are lies we tell ourselves; the truth is far less harsh – having pain does not necessarily mean your whole day is ruined, your colleagues won't think that you are not pulling your weight because you reschedule a meeting and just because you haven't found something to help you with the pain so far does not mean that managing your pain through controlling your thoughts will not help either.

Think back to the last time you had pain. What unhelpful thought did you have? If that thought comes back again, you can recognise it for what it is and it will be less likely that you will engage with it and let it ruin your mood or your plans.

Peter

> Peter has early-onset Parkinson's disease and although he does not experience many Parkinson's symptoms, he frequently gets an intense pain in his shoulder and stiffness in his neck. Pain relief

medication did not offer much respite, so Peter was trying to distract himself by working, watching TV or playing video games when he was feeling pain.

However, distraction was not always successful and sometimes he found it difficult to concentrate on other activities when in pain. He decided to join our mindfulness course. One of the exercises we did in the course was to focus on the pain and explore the physical sensation of the pain. Where is the pain? Does it move around or stay in the same place? Does pain intensity change? How does the pain feel, burning, stabbing, stinging etc? The idea was that without judging or qualifying the pain to stay with it and explore it with kindness and curiosity.

Naturally, Peter hated the exercise. Who wouldn't? He said the pain was getting worse and worse as he was focusing on it. Despite how much he disliked the exercise, he agreed to experiment with it again in the next sessions. When at home, watching television worked most of the time as a distraction from the pain but he wanted to try something different for the times when not even TV could distract him. In the fourth session, he observed that when noticing the pain, his mind played out all sorts of unpleasant scenarios, about how bad this is, that the pain is debilitating that he can't go on suffering like that. It happened very quickly, his mind flicking between noticing the pain and having thoughts about the 'badness' of the situation. That was his breakthrough. He saw how the mind was intruding and making things worse. The pain was present, and he could do very little about it, but he could let the thoughts about pain go.

After Peter noticed his thoughts and started practising letting them go without identifying with them too much, we added another step to the exercise. As well as the pain, I asked him to notice other things for example, his breath and the fact that he is breathing or the sounds around him. By the end of the 8-week course, Peter was able to widen and narrow his attentional focus while staying with the painful sensation. Being able to focus on other things without ignoring the pain opened up more choices and give him more freedom. He can now choose what he wants to do, not just do the things that will distract him from pain.

Being aware of your thoughts, emotions and coping mechanisms and their potential effects on your pain level is a good start in your pain management journey. Staying connected to your personal values and goals can help you disengage from these unhelpful thoughts.

Watching television, exercising, reading or engaging in other pleasant non-demanding activities could help distract from the pain. When reducing the pain or getting rid of the pain is beyond our control, distraction might be the most beneficial way to cope with the pain. There are situations though that distraction is not as helpful. Peter sometimes did not want to watch TV, he wanted to cook dinner or play with his kids, but doing anything physical reminded him of his shoulder pain and was not a sufficient distraction. Staying with the pain in this more accepting and open way gave him the options to do other things in the evenings. Research evidence further supports the notion that accepting the pain can be a useful pain management technique.[8] By accepting the pain, we eliminate a layer of suffering (the unpleasant thoughts that usually accompany the pain), and also instead of spending time and energy ignoring the pain, we let the pain be while directing our attention to whatever we intend to do.

By accepting the pain, it is less likely that you will try to avoid thoughts around pain or avoid engaging in physical activity or other activities you value. Research has also shown that diverting attention away from painful stimuli can be unhelpful.

Mindfulness, i.e. being aware of the present moment without too much emotional reaction or judgement, can be very helpful when managing pain. Paradoxically focusing on pain sensation and trying to transform sensation or adopting 'distanced observer role' is more promising.[9] Mindfulness makes the brain react differently to pain stimuli. Researchers at Wake Forest School of Medicine have found that people who are naturally more mindful felt less pain compared to people who were not as mindful inclined. Seventy-six healthy volunteers who had never meditated first completed the Freiburg Mindfulness Inventory, a reliable clinical measurement of mindfulness, to determine their baseline levels. Then, while undergoing functional magnetic resonance imaging, they were administered painful heat stimulation (49° C).

Whole brain analyses revealed that the volunteers with the higher mindfulness tendencies showed greater deactivation of a brain region called the posterior cingulate cortex, a central neural node of the default mode network, during painful heat. Further, in those that reported higher pain, people with higher mindfulness ratings had less activation in the central nodes (posterior cingulate cortex) of the default network and experienced less pain. Those with lower mindfulness ratings had greater activation of this part of the brain and also felt more pain.

The default mode network extends from the posterior cingulate cortex to the medial prefrontal cortex of the brain. These two brain regions continuously feed information back and forth. This network is associated with processing feelings of self and mind wandering. As soon as you start performing a task, the connection between these two brain regions in the default mode network disengages and the brain allocates information and processes to other neural areas. In other words, the more mindful volunteers were less caught up in the experience of pain, which was associated with lower pain reports.[10]

Even if you are not blessed with a more mindful disposition, fear not. Research evidence have shown that your mindfulness skills can increase significantly after a short mindfulness course (typically 8 weeks).

Physical activity (aerobic, muscle strengthening, flexibility training and movement therapy) in appropriate frequency, duration and intensity can also improve pain severity, physical function and consequent quality of life.[11,12] Even though there are no strict guidelines, frequent movement is better than sedentary behaviour. The best approach is to talk to your healthcare team to help you tailor physical activity to your needs, limitations and resources.

To summarise, becoming aware of your thought distortions so they won't highjack your mood, using distractions as long as they are helpful and they don't also distract you from things you value, focusing on the physical sensations of pain while removing emotions and thoughts around the pain (through mindfulness training) and appropriate levels and types of physical activity are all techniques that scientific evidence shows to work when managing pain.

Pain diary

To get a clear understanding of how your mood, activities and conditions affect your pain, keep a diary. You can begin by recording your activities and pain levels three times a day, at regular intervals.

Date/time	Situation	Pain (0 – no pain to 10 – excruciating pain)	Notes on pain	Emotional distress (0 – no distress to 10 – severely distressed)	Notes on emotions	Response
17/8/19, 10 a.m.	Watching TV	5	Deep aching pain in my left lower back	3	I felt angry and wanted to shout	Asked my wife to give me a massage. It alleviated the pain only for a short time.

Look for patterns. For example, is the pain worse after sitting for a long time? Is it less when you are engaged in a favourite hobby? How much do you notice pain? This can give you good data on things that you could modify to prevent your pain from worsening. For example if you notice that pain is particularly bad a certain time of day, check whether there is something that also happens at that time that might have something to do with the exaggerated pain.

How much you notice pain can vary according to your mood, fatigue and muscle tension. It's important to distinguish between physical pain sensations, such as stabbing, burning and aching and emotional pain distress, and the accompanying emotions of anger, anxiety, frustration, or sadness. This is useful because even if your physical pain may not be reduced, you can feel better about the pain and consequently experience less distress, anxiety, helplessness and despair.

Fatigue control

Fatigue is a common complaint among people with long-term conditions, especially, neurological conditions,[13] cancer survivors[14] and inflammatory related conditions.[15]

One of the reasons fatigue is such a common symptom for long-term conditions is that the illness itself, no matter what the illness is, demands more energy. The energy that would have supported everyday activities is now used to heal the body. In response your body will release chemical signals to conserve energy and make you rest more.

People dealing with a complex long-term condition like cancer, Multiple Sclerosis, or stroke often rate fatigue as the most debilitating symptom of their condition. Fatigue associated with a long-term condition is different to any experienced before; the intensity of fatigue is overwhelming and the trajectory uncertain.[16] Fatigue also impacts sleep and contributes to sleep disturbances that complicate things further. Fatigue may be the most common symptom responsible for higher levels of distress and lower quality of life.

Sometimes pressure strain and stress can also be confused with fatigue. If you feel under pressure, the strain will increase the likelihood that the pressure turns into stress and stress can often lead to exacerbation of fatigue. By learning to discern between fatigue, strain, pressure and stress, you naturally increase your capacity to handle fatigue skilfully. For example, if you see that you're on the verge of strain, you might decide not to do certain things that would push you over. A lot of the times even when we are doing enough, we might feel that we haven't achieved much. Keeping a log of small daily wins or achievement at the end of each day or even starting the day with a list of things you achieved the previous day instead of a standard to-do list will help with boosting your confidence and reducing your stress that can consecutively contribute to fatigue.

Figuring out what exacerbates fatigue can help you find the best way to combat it. Inactivity is a common cause of fatigue in long-term conditions. Muscles that are not used become de-conditioned and less efficient at doing what they are supposed to do. Poor nutrition can be another reason. Food that is inferior quality or not consumed in the appropriate quantities will not give the body the appropriate fuel to work. For tips on improving your diet and activity levels, go to Chapter 6. Sleep difficulties, another common symptom shared among various long-term conditions, can also lead to increased feelings of fatigue. See next section on sleep difficulties and how to manage them.

Feeling stressed, anxious or depressed is closely linked to feeling tired. The previous chapter discussed some of the psychological difficulties and how to overcome them. Finally, your medication can also lead to feeling fatigued. If you notice fatigue after taking a particular medicine, discuss with your doctor whether there is an alternative or whether you can alter the dosage.

Steve

Before his Multiple Sclerosis diagnosis, Steve was a long-distance runner and cyclist. He worked 12-hour days at a research lab and in his free time he was training and competing in running races or cycled with his friends. Knowing how to handle fatigue and pain after all the years of long-distance running, he never expected that he would struggle with fatigue as much as he did lately.

He had spent the last few days intensively researching car modifications – his latest project, visiting car dealers and meeting up with other people with Multiple Sclerosis to ask about how they modified their cars. He worked intensely on this project. This was the only way he knew how to work. Intensely, with no breaks, aiming high and investigating all possibilities.

On the 'good' days, when Steve experienced less fatigue, he crammed in all the activities that he couldn't manage when his fatigue was more severe. However, by doing more than he was used to his pain was stirred up later in the day. The following day his fatigue would get worse, so he would spend the day resting and doing very little, much to his annoyance and frustration. After a day or so like this, his energy levels would increase again, and the pattern would be repeated. He didn't want to give in to the fatigue and he didn't want anyone to think he wasn't trying. There was a gap between what he wanted to achieve and what he managed to do each day and that gap was a constant source of frustration.

Having all or nothing type of behavioural patterns can also add to experiencing fatigue. Commonly, on the days people have more energy they try to cram in everything they can. And as you can imagine, this leads to energy crashing. Even though you feel you are achieving a lot during the 'good' days, following the intense activity you're left feeling lethargic and depleted. To increase the amount of stuff you can achieve despite your fatigue is to practise pacing. Start with doing things that you can comfortably manage without exerting yourself and build up from there slowly. The key word here is consistency. Plan to do a little but every day.

To begin with, work out your starting point, what you can manage comfortably now. To 'pace-up' an activity you should plan to do a bit more each day or every second day. Each increase should be small, and you should not do more than you planned, even if you feel like it. It also helps if you break up larger tasks into smaller steps. Create a list of all the smaller steps and based on how much you can manage now and your 'pace-up' rate create a rough timeline of completion.

Recording your progress can be very motivating. It's also essential to take frequent, quick breaks. Do something for a set amount of time – 15 minutes is a good length of time – then take a break – then do a bit more – then take another brief break – and so on. Evidence suggests that Cognitive Behavioural Therapy, graded exercise,[17] mindfulness training[18,19] and sleep and stress management[13] can improve symptoms of fatigue.

In cognitive behavioural therapy, you will be working with your therapist identifying unhelpful thoughts and finding ways to modify these thoughts, so they won't hold you back. Graded exercise involves physical activity that increases in intensity. Mindfulness training is based on daily meditation practices that aim to increase your present moment awareness, acceptance and self-compassion. Sleep and stress management training includes techniques that I discussed in the previous chapter (stress management, pp 67–74) and I will discuss further in the next section (sleep training).

A common ingredient that is included in these interventions is working on fear avoidance of beliefs and behaviours.[20] Repetitive thoughts and emotions like fear and anger can fatigue the mind and avoiding physical movement can further fatigue the body.

Magda

Magda is a senior psychologist working at a busy University hospital. On top of seeing patients in the clinic, she is heading the training program for clinical psychologists and she delivers lectures for the program. She never recognised her fatigue as a symptom of her Parkinson's but put it down to bad time management or stress. Therefore, she always assumed it was something transient that didn't need addressing. It was years of struggling with her energy levels before she decided to tackle her fatigue as a symptom that won't go away unless she gets proactive.

She paid attention to her thoughts and every time she had a self-critical thought, she would move the rubber band she was wearing on her wrist from one wrist to the other. Moving the rubber band made her aware of her thoughts and stopped them from escalating.

She also planned her days more carefully. She wanted a multi-faceted life so to avoid neglecting any area she planned her clinic work, university work, house chores, holidays, social activities, family activities and exercise separately, and made sure that during the week she would spend some time on each. She broke bigger work projects into smaller parts and only committed to doing a little every day. She spread the things she had to do over the weekly period and tried not to do more than what she had planned. For example, she wanted to address clinical psychology trainees' most frequent questions in a shared document to better support the trainees and save herself time in the future. She wanted to have the document ready for the next academic year starting in September. Having a deadline and a specific goal, she was able to break it down into small actionable steps, making achieving the goal more realistic and less overwhelming.

She also realised that her current caseload in the clinic was beyond her abilities on the days that fatigue was especially bad, and she negotiated with her line manager a smaller caseload.

During the weekends, she loved quilting, but she got so absorbed in it that she did not take any breaks, resulting in her fatigue getting worse and not being able to quilt for weeks. So, she set herself a time limit and set a timer to take a break to stretch her legs every 15 minutes.

Small and big tweaks like that helped Magda to better manage her fatigue and feel more in control of her life.

To summarise, things you can do to help manage your fatigue include finding out what exacerbates the fatigue and take care of the causes, like stress, sleep, exercise and nutrition. Further, look into your all-or-nothing behaviours and try to avoid the 'catching-up-on-all-the-things-when-you-can' trap. Research evidence also suggests giving cognitive behavioural therapy, graded exercise and stress management a try.

Anatomy of a good night's sleep

A lot of people report not sleeping well or not feeling rested when they wake up, but this vague sense of restlessness can be narrowed to the specific issues with sleep. Several sleep experts[21] reviewed more than 200 previously published sleep studies in an attempt to define more concretely what sort of sleep people should aspire to each night. A paper in *Sleep Health* outlined the four main principles of sleep: 1. You take half an hour or less to fall asleep. 2. You wake up no more than once per night. 3. If you do wake up in the middle of the night, you fall back asleep within 20 minutes. 4. You are asleep for at least 85% of the time you spend in bed.

Alas, a goodnight sleep doesn't always happen. And when it doesn't happen it's not that big a deal. Be compassionate and patient: it takes time and by being kind and relaxed around your sleep habits you remove unnecessary obstacles.

You can let go of worries about sleep and improve your sleep with a three-part strategy:

- Enjoy your day
- Prepare for a relaxing night, and
- Stop the struggle.

Let's look at each in turn.

Enjoy your day

First of all, let's move the focus away from the night's sleep and on to how you spend the day. A day that is relatively busy and enjoyable with the right number of relaxing breaks is more likely to produce enough 'sleep drive' to lead to a good night's sleep. Whenever thoughts like "I feel really tired", "I didn't get enough sleep" or "I can't find energy to do anything" pop into your mind, pause, acknowledge them and let them go without too much lingering. Not sleeping well will make you less energetic the next day but most of the time the mind exacerbates the effects by focusing too much on this. OK, you did not have a great night, that was that, what can you do today to make the day fun?

A great way to enjoy your day is to plan it in advance. Of course, there will be things that need to be done or that need sorting out, trips to the shops that you haven't planned etc but having planned from the previous night three to five 'main' events will guide your day. The events could be something like going to the supermarket to pick up healthy snacks, walking your dog around the park or sampling cakes at the newly opened café in your neighbourhood – enough to get you moving, out of the house, experiencing things and interacting with other people.

Isabelle found her days really overwhelming as she was unable to do any simple task without a great amount of struggle and pain. She told me she always planned to do one 'big thing' a day – something like taking her car to the garage or picking up her grandson from nursery and spending an hour with him until her daughter-in-law would come to pick him up. The one task a day was her focus and she would be very satisfied to tick it off. But she had some smaller tasks that she included in her daily list just for the thrill of ticking things off. The smaller tasks included things like taking the bins out or cleaning the cat's food bowl.

No matter how you decide to plan your day, make sure your overall week includes some tasks that make you feel effective and productive and give you a sense of achievement and some tasks that are enjoyable, this way your days and weeks will feel happy and satisfying.

If your condition varies a lot from day to day and unpredictability and uncertainty make planning difficult, you can use an altered version of daily planning. It might mean that you create a bucket list of things you would like to do or achieve and depending on how you feel each day you can pick up an item to do. Your list might include items that can be completed in a few minutes and others that will take most of the day. Take each day as it comes. The point is not to treat your bucket list as an infinite to-do list that will never get done, but as an ideas bucket list of things you like to do, so you can bring more intention to your days.

Equally important is to integrate some resting time during the day. Have an active, alive home with music and TV and chatter and activity, indoors and outdoors but include resting times as well. It might be that a rhythm of an hour and a half productivity followed by a 15-minute break for three cycles followed by 2-hour break and another three cycles of an hour and a half activity and a 15-minute break will work for you or a variation of such a rhythm. The timings are not important here; what is important is to construct your day to a rhythm that will feel easy and natural to you.

Prepare for a relaxing night

Prepare yourself and your environment to wind down the day and relax. Don't focus on the sleep itself, just start winding things down. It is best to keep a similar routine every day, similar timings and similar activities, so both your mind and your body get into a pattern over time. For example, reading a book in low light; having a warm bath; having a warm drink of milk or herbal tea; avoiding electronic devices or socialising for an hour or two before you go to bed; avoiding strenuous physical activity before you go to bed – even though physical activity during the day can help you regulate your sleep and help you go to sleep easier at night, doing something really vigorous just before bed will not be conducive to a good night's sleep. You may also want to ensure that the environment is relatively dark and peaceful.

When facilitating a group of people with Parkinson's disease we talked about sleep and people shared things that helped them feel comfortable, relaxed and peaceful in the evenings before bed. Here are some ideas of things you could include in your winding down routine. Ian swore by a pair of fresh pyjamas of breathable material; his issue was that he was getting sweaty in the night and that woke him up and then it was difficult to get back to sleep. So, a new pair of lighter and more breathable fabric pyjamas did the trick. Alexa and Louisa talked about melatonin tablets that you can purchase over the counter. Melatonin is a natural hormone that the brain produces in the late evening and throughout the night. According to a research published in *Clinical Pharmacology & Therapeutics*, melatonin tablets could help when taken several hours before bedtime.[22] Alexa and Louisa also talked about using a 'light box', which is basically a lamp that turns slowly on and off when programmed. During the winter, in countries where the natural light is limited, our circadian rhythm can be affected and so does our sleep. Having this artificial light mimicking daylight can help the body to distinguish between day and night and adjust appropriately. Having regular massages was Pamela's tip to stay relaxed and sleep better. Massages can be expensive and feel too self-indulgent, but we are all allowed a few things on our 'luxuries' list, things that are somewhat expensive but make us feel happy and abundant, and Pamela was adamant that getting a massage was improving her quality of life and quality of sleep. Think about all the little things you spend money on that you don't really need or want, she said; you could instead spend it on something that you really like and enjoy. And it doesn't have to be too frequent and you can find coupons and promotional deals to get massages for cheaper. Other practical tips that were mentioned during the session included to avoid drinking too much water before bed, avoid caffeine and alcohol and avoid screens after 8 p.m.

Having a few techniques that you know can help you relax is very useful but relying too much on them can also bring the opposite effects. In his brilliantly written and informative book, *The sleep book, how to sleep well every night*,[23] Dr Guy Meadows urges his reader to let go of unnecessary sleep props but also don't give up all the props but adopt a balanced approach to sleep. Don't get hooked up on rigid sleep routines and rituals, he warns. Sleep is a natural and individualised thing. Take time, try different things to see what works for you. Usually sleep happens when you stop the struggle.

Stop the struggle

An easy trap that a lot of us fall into, even when we know that we mustn't think or stress about something, is that we do and then we stress even more in a vicious cycle that escalates indefinitely. Of course, you will worry about not sleeping, and you will wonder about how it will negatively affect your day, there is no escaping that. The real challenge is – can you be OK with having these worrisome thoughts? Don't indulge them, just look at them and nod as if talking to them and saying: Cool, I see you've come again but I don't have time to chat, I'd like to do something else.

First, worrying about how bad your sleep has been or imagining how bad things will be in the future if you don't sleep only helps to increase night-time arousal/wakefulness levels. Cognitive behavioural therapy has been empirically tested as a treatment of insomnia and found effective in reducing different sleep-related problems for people who only experience sleep difficulties[24] and people for whom sleep difficulties are derived from chronic pain due to cancer, back pain, arthritis, or fibromyalgia.[25] In cognitive behavioural therapy people are encouraged to identify, challenge and replace dysfunctional beliefs and attitudes about sleep and insomnia. Such misconceptions may include unrealistic expectations of sleep, fear of missing out on sleep and overestimation of the consequences of poor sleep.

But how could you 'Get a good night's sleep'? The best you can do to improve your sleep is to stop focusing on your lack of sleep. The brain is a problem-solving machine. When the problem is 'difficulty sleeping' the brain will get on overdrive trying to sort out this problem and all this brain activity will keep you awake all night. It is a bit like carrying a full cup of coffee on a tray, the more you look at the cup and not where you are going the more likely it is to spill the coffee. The more relaxed you are about it the more likely it is for the coffee to remain in the cup.

Jon Kabat-Zinn in his book *Full Catastrophe Living, How to cope with stress, pain and illness using mindfulness meditation*, talks about his own insomnia that he stopped seeing as an issue and started seeing as an opportunity to catch up on his writing or practice mindfulness meditation. Mindfulness meditation helps to acknowledge your thoughts and not let them bother you but go on and do what you want to do despite what your thoughts are saying. In the night you can use the sensation of your duvet touching your toes or the gentle movement of your chest as you breathe to ground yourself in the present moment and a place to return your attention when your mind wants to wander off. You can't stop your mind from having worrisome thoughts, but you can always choose how much you buy into them.

Another way to catch those thoughts that keep you awake is to write them down in a journal. Marcus Aurelius, the Roman Emperor from 161 to 180 AD, recorded every night his thoughts on what he had learned during the day, reflected on the daily events and wrote his ideas on what he saw and heard. These notes serve as a source of self-guidance and self-improvement. There is a lot to be said about the way we currently live our lives without a moment to really reflect on things and form our own opinions – but I digress. Writing down our thoughts can be a great way to process things; it is also a way to recognise our thoughts and put them out of our mind and on paper. And if what you are writing happens to be about anxious thoughts it's important to move the notebook out of sight when you are done, as a study published in *Psychological Science* showed treating thoughts as material objects can increase or decrease their impact,[26] so if you write your thoughts and you keep the paper with you, it will act as a physical reminder and if you throw it away it will feel as if you have also discarded the thoughts it contains.

A few more tips for a good night's sleep:

- Napping during the day can reduce the amount of sleep you get at night.
- Strengthen your unconscious association between your bedroom and sleep. Many people who report problems with insomnia also perform other activities while sitting in bed – they watch movies, work on the computer, make calls and even eat meals. Bed is only to be used for sleeping and sex.
- Make your bedroom a fully dark, quiet, cool, comfortable space to help you to fall asleep.
- Before bed avoid bright lights – especially lights with blue hues to them – for several hours before bedtime. Bright white incandescent or fluorescent lights are bad; computer screens and LED television screens are even worse. The blue-frequency light greatly reduces your brain's release of melatonin.
- On the flip side, when you wake up first thing in the morning, you should look out the window at the blue sky and when this is possible you can stare at a computer screen or television. Broad-spectrum or bluish illumination, especially bright

illumination, will reset your internal clock and get your brain active and on its way.

Blueprint for tackling symptoms

Long-term conditions cannot be cured but a lot of the symptoms can be managed. Your body is your personal forest. What is the weather in your forest? What creatures live in the forest? Some are fearsome, some are kind and considerate. Some are understated but essential to the viability of the forest. Sounds strange but bear with me. Experiment with thinking about your condition in this alternative way to map out symptoms and unique characteristics of your condition. Write down a description of your personal forest with all the challenges and delights, the nooks yet to be explored and the unexplained phenomena.

Louise

Louise lives in a very charming part of UK. She insisted I should visit her and not conduct the interview over the phone because she wanted to show me her garden and her town. I was actually quite giddy to visit her and that part of the country. Her house was as charming as I was imagining it to be. Wisteria covering the facade made it difficult to find out where the door was. It was like a house from a fairy tale. Standing in front of the door, waiting for Louise to answer it I could smell cinnamon and sugar. Something delicious was in the oven. She had told me she'd bake her favourite cookies for me. The door opened and a smiley Louise gave me a bear hug even though our communication thus far was limited to a couple of emails to arrange the visit and a phone call to ask for directions, as I lost my way walking to her place from the train station.

Louise is in her mid-forties. She's never married and had no children – the opportunity never came up, she explained. She lives on her own but her mother and sister live close by. She cares for her mother who had suffered a stroke a couple of years ago and helps out her sister sometimes who has fibromyalgia, which occasionally leaves her completely bed-ridden for days. Louise was diagnosed with lupus in her late teens and Multiple Sclerosis in her late twenties but since then she had also been diagnosed with four different types of cancer. At the time I met her she was recovering from her latest cancer treatment.

I felt so welcomed in Louise's home. She was a very gregarious small woman with a big smile. Apart from her culinary skills, I was also amazed by her organisational and planning skills, once we started to talk about how she balances everything that is going on in her life. She worked as an office manager. She was the first employee of the company and as the company grew to a 40-person operation she was the one that managed all the operations side of the business and helped the company grow. Her boss was very understanding of the adjustments needed to be made to accommodate her needs. He was happy to keep the job as flexible as Louise wanted since she was essential to the company. However, five years ago Louise decided she could no longer work and left the company.

She applied her skills managing paperwork in the office to her personal life as well. She showed me a cabinet marked 'Life admin' with folders that contained correspondence, test results, medication prescriptions etc. Separate folders were dedicated for separate conditions. She also had an always-updating document with the conditions, when she was diagnosed, what medication she was on and her allergies. This way, she explained, I don't have to remember all of these when I go to the hospital or see a new GP, I just hand them the document.

'I like setting goals, and the same goes with keeping symptoms and medical treatments under control', she told me. She did not set goals like being able to walk around the neighbourhood without a walking stick or cook dinner every night standing, as she did not have control over those goals. Her goals were more around consistency, learning new things and creating her own ways to cope with symptoms. Louise had three current goals that she was working on at the moment: 1. Stay up to date with new research regarding Multiple Sclerosis and Lupus and ways to cope with symptoms. 2. Be consistent with her treatment. She was taking antidepressant medication to help her with her fatigue and previously was taking it sporadically, but now she wanted to take the medication consistently to determine whether it works for her or not. 3. Attend the social meet-ups organised by the local Multiple Sclerosis group. Attending those meeting required a lot of effort and as an introvert she always preferred to stay in and read books to going out and meeting and talking to new people but frequently she'd gathered unexpected good information attending these meet-ups.

Having a good understanding of her condition, organising the information and setting targets of how best to manage things all helped Louise to feel more in control of her condition.

If you have followed and completed the activities in Chapter 2, you'd probably have a list of your symptoms that you would like to tackle and prioritise the ones you'd like to address first. The first call of action is to talk to your medical team about them and get some advice on how they can be resolved. It is not uncommon for symptoms to be left untreated, just because it is uncomfortable talking about them with a health professional.

Embarrassment and difficulties with the vocabulary to use for certain sensitive symptoms, such as sexual dysfunction, are also common.[27] Symptoms like sexual difficulties (erection, vaginal dryness), incontinence and problems with concentration and memory can be experienced in silence. Most of those symptoms can be better managed with health professional advice, medications or non-pharmaceutical interventions. And yet people will not report them.

You might be thinking that this does not relate to you, you are generally comfortable talking to your medical team about any health concerns you have and yet some symptoms remain unreported because you simply might not think they are related to your condition or side effects of your medication. Pain and sleep problems are commonly perceived as not part of long-term neurological conditions. Bowel and bladder symptoms might often simply be accepted as part of getting old. So, the first step is to recognise the symptoms of the condition, then find the appropriate health care professional to discuss these.

First, identify the most troubling symptoms for you and talk to your medical team about your options and what best to do. You can then supplement this step by doing your own research. Visit relevant forums to see what others say and do, look into informative articles on your symptoms or even find out and read accounts of others' stories. It can give you some ideas of ways to cope or things you can do differently. You can also attend local groups, conferences, open days and conventions related to your condition. Once you start digging around you will be surprised by all the different things that go on and are relevant to your condition.

Armed with self-awareness and knowledge you can come up with your own plan and set your goals of living well. What actions will move you towards a better quality of life? Which symptoms do you want to manage and in which way? To avoid feeling overwhelmed, choose the most troubling symptom that you would like to address first or the one that you feel most confident addressing. Build your symptom management skills towards tackling more challenging symptoms that require more complex solutions.

Now let's look in more detail how exactly you can transform your best intentions to make changes into actionable reality.

Action plan for dealing with symptoms

As the saying goes, a goal without a plan is just a wish. By planning you can form a vivid image on how you want things to go. Having this active image in your mind will help you act accordingly when it is required and prevent you from forgetting or slipping into previous habits you want to change.[28] Something planned can be executed effectively and immediately.

To begin with, the plan won't be linked to your ultimate goal (e.g. have more energy) but to the chosen behaviour (e.g. increase exercise) that will serve the goal. Therefore, consider ways to increase physical activity by maybe pacing in the room while talking on the phone, walking short distances instead of using the car, joining a health club or gym etc.

Ensuring that you stick to your plan on how to deal with your symptoms is not complex but requires two steps that are crucial for the success of the plans.

The plan

Example:

> In order to deal with my frequent falls, I need to do balance exercises.
> I will do my balance exercises twice a week, on Saturday and Sunday morning after breakfast, for 15 minutes each time.
> I will do my exercises in the living room, while watching the morning news.
> To do my exercises I will follow the instructions and the 'how to' photos on the NHS website.

To avoid premature and unrealistic plans to deal with symptoms, you need time and resources. For the preceding example, you will need time to talk to your doctor about balance activities and read through the guidelines on the NHS website. You will need to commit giving up 30 minutes a week to doing your exercises. You will need a computer or a way to print the instructions of the activities or write them down on a notebook that you can consult when it is time to do your exercises.

Now, your turn:

In order to deal with _____ I need to _____

When: _____

Where: _____

How: _____

The Plan B

OK, now you have a plan of what you need to do, where, when and how to put your intentions into action. However, the power of habits, other goals and life circumstances can interfere with the execution of your plans. Having a Plan B in your back pocket can help overcome anticipated barriers. What situations, times or places do you anticipate it will be more likely for you to abandon your plans?

A great way to create your Plan B is to use a technique that psychologists call implementation intentions. Implementation intentions are where a person specifies when, where and how they will perform a particular behaviour, linking the 'when' and 'where' to the 'how' using an 'If . . . then . . .' structure.[28,29] For example, 'If I am in the kitchen and I have just finished eating my lunch, then I will select a piece of fruit to eat for dessert'. Implementation intentions are thought to work by helping people more easily identify good opportunities to act when they encounter them.[30] They also increase the chances that you will conduct this behaviour automatically.[31] In other words to make this behaviour a habit. This is very helpful because it saves you mental energy, makes it is less likely you will find excuses not to do what you intended to do and keeps you motivated.

There is substantial evidence to indicate that implementation intentions can be a very effective way of changing behaviour.[32] There is also evidence that tell us when these implementation intentions become even more successful. For example, when the behaviour you want to change is easy[33] and the current behaviour you want to change is not a habit, i.e. you don't perform it automatically, without thinking.[34] There is also evidence to show that implementation intentions will only be helpful when you are motivated to perform the behaviour.[35,36]

Plan Bs need to be as detailed as first-line planning and the barriers must be specific situations, times or places that you are more likely to abandon your plans. Think about subjective barriers that you can control and change, or interactions with others. For example, feeling fatigued might be difficult to control and change but how you react to fatigue can be controlled, how much control you let fatigue have over your day is something that you can change. A few examples of Plan Bs:

> **If** I have plans to meet friends for breakfast in the weekend, **then** I will do my balance exercises the night before, before I go to bed.
>
> **If** my morning feels too busy and hectic to do the exercises, **then** I will do my exercises as soon as I get out of bed, before getting dressed or having breakfast.
>
> **If** my daughter interrupts my morning exercises, **then** I will ask my husband to distract her for the 15 minutes I need to complete my exercises.

If _____ (Barrier 1) happens, then

_____ (Plan B)

If _____ (Barrier 2) happens, then

_____ (Plan B)

If _____ (Barrier 3) happens, then

_____ (Plan B)

To summarise: Plan A lays out the strategy, Plan B keeps you in target course and away from distractions. For Plan A you need to have enough knowledge about your symptoms, how best to manage it and what will likely work for you. For second-line planning, you need experience. There might be some barriers like lack of time or interference of other symptoms that you can anticipate and plan around but while you manage your symptoms following your plan you will identify other distractions and eventually you will create all the appropriate Plan Bs to keep you on target.

Bibliography

1 McCracken LM, Gutiérrez-Martínez O. Processes of Change in Psychological Flexibility in an Interdisciplinary Group-Based Treatment for Chronic Pain Based on Acceptance and Commitment Therapy.

Behaviour Research and Therapy. 2011;49(4):267–274. doi:10.1016/j. brat.2011.02.004

2 McCracken LM, Evon D, Karapas ET. Satisfaction with Treatment for Chronic Pain in a Specialty Service: Preliminary Prospective Results. *European Journal of Pain*. 2002;6(5):387–393. doi:10.1016/ S1090-3801(02)00042-3

3 Wicksell RK, Olsson GL, Hayes SC. Psychological Flexibility as a Mediator of Improvement in Acceptance and Commitment Therapy for Patients with Chronic Pain Following Whiplash. *European Journal of Pain*. 2010;14(10):1059.e1–1059.e11. doi:10.1016/j.ejpain. 2010.05.001

4 Wicksell RK, Ahlqvist J, Bring A, Melin L, Olsson GL. Can Exposure and Acceptance Strategies Improve Functioning and Life Satisfaction in People with Chronic Pain and Whiplash-Associated Disorders (WAD)? A Randomized Controlled Trial. *Cognitive Behaviour Therapy*. 2008;37(3):169–182. doi:10.1080/16506070802078970

5 Wright MA, Wren AA, Somers TJ, et al. Pain Acceptance, Hope, and Optimism: Relationships to Pain and Adjustment in Patients with Chronic Musculoskeletal Pain. *Journal of Pain*. 2011;12(11):1155–1162. doi:10.1016/j.jpain.2011.06.002

6 Leeuw M, Goossens MEJB, Linton SJ, Crombez G, Boersma K, Vlaeyen JWS. The Fear-Avoidance Model of Musculoskeletal Pain: Current State of Scientific Evidence. *Journal of Behavioral Medicine*. 2007;30(1):77–94. doi:10.1007/s10865-006-9085-0

7 Vlaeyen JWS, Linton SJ. Fear-Avoidance Model of Chronic Musculoskeletal Pain: 12 Years on. *Pain*. 2012;153(6):1144–1147. doi:10.1016/j. pain.2011.12.009

8 Harrison AM, Bogosian A, Silber E, McCracken LM, Moss-Morris R. "It Feels Like Someone Is Hammering My Feet": Understanding Pain and Its Management from the Perspective of People with Multiple Sclerosis. *Multiple Sclerosis*. 2015;21(4). doi:10.1177/1352458514544538

9 Graham CJ, Brown SL, Horne AW. The Importance of Pain Imagery in Women with Endometriosis-Associated Pain, and Wider Implications for Patients with Chronic Pain. In: *Meanings of Pain*. Springer International Publishing; 2019:117–141. doi:10.1007/978-3-030-24154-4_7

10 Zeidan F, Salomons T, Farris SR, et al. Neural Mechanisms Supporting the Relationship between Dispositional Mindfulness and Pain. *Pain*. 2018;159(12):2477–2485. doi:10.1097/j.pain.0000000000001344

11 Geneen LJ, Moore RA, Clarke C, Martin D, Colvin LA, Smith BH. Physical Activity and Exercise for Chronic Pain in Adults: An Overview of Cochrane Reviews. *Cochrane Database of Systematic Review*. 2017;2017(4). doi:10.1002/14651858.CD011279.pub3

12 Ambrose KR, Golightly YM. Physical Exercise as Non-Pharmacological Treatment of Chronic Pain: Why and When. *Best Practice and Research:*

Clinical Rheumatology. 2015;29(1):120–130. doi:10.1016/j.berh.2015. 04.022

13 De Groot MH, Phillips SJ, Eskes GA. Fatigue Associated with Stroke and Other Neurologic Conditions: Implications for Stroke Rehabilitation. *Archives of Physical Medicine and Rehabilitation.* 2003; 84(11):1714–1720. doi:10.1053/S0003-9993(03)00346-0

14 Bower JE, Ganz PA, Desmond KA, et al. Fatigue in Long-Term Breast Carcinoma Survivors: A Longitudinal Investigation. *Cancer.* 2006; 106(4):751–758. doi:10.1002/cncr.21671

15 Overman CL, Kool MB, Da Silva JAP, Geenen R. The Prevalence of Severe Fatigue in Rheumatic Diseases: An International Study. *Clinical Rheumatology.* 2016;35(2):409–415. doi:10.1007/s10067-015-3035-6

16 Whitehead LC, Unahi K, Burrell B, Crowe MT. The Experience of Fatigue across Long-Term Conditions: A Qualitative Meta-Synthesis. *Journal of Pain and Symptom Management.* 2016;52(1):131–143.e1. doi:10.1016/j.jpainsymman.2016.02.013

17 White PD, Goldsmith K, Johnson AL, et al. Comparison of Adaptive Pacing Therapy, Cognitive Behaviour Therapy, Graded Exercise Therapy, and Specialist Medical Care for Chronic Fatigue Syndrome (PACE): A Randomised Trial. *The Lancet.* 2011;377(9768):823–836. doi:10.1016/S0140-6736(11)60096-2

18 Johansson B, Bjuhr H, Rönnbäck L. Mindfulness-Based Stress Reduction (MBSR) Improves Long-Term Mental Fatigue after Stroke or Traumatic Brain Injury. *Brain Injury.* 2012;26(13–14):1621–1628. doi: 10.3109/02699052.2012.700082

19 Nejati S, Rajezi Esfahani S, Rahmani S, Afrookhteh G, Hoveida S. The Effect of Group Mindfulness-Based Stress Reduction and Consciousness Yoga Program on Quality of Life and Fatigue Severity in Patients with MS. *Journal of Caring Science.* 2016;5(4):325–335. doi:10.15171/jcs.2016.034

20 Chalder T, Goldsmith KA, White PD, Sharpe M, Pickles AR. Rehabilitative Therapies for Chronic Fatigue Syndrome: A Secondary Mediation Analysis of the PACE Trial. *The Lancet Psychiatry.* 2015;2(2):141–152. doi:10.1016/S2215-0366(14)00069-8

21 Ohayon M, Wickwire EM, Hirshkowitz M, et al. National Sleep Foundation's Sleep Quality Recommendations: First Report. *Sleep Health.* 2017;3(1):6–19. doi:10.1016/j.sleh.2016.11.006

22 Zhdanova IV, Wurtman RJ, Lynch HJ, et al. Sleep-Inducing Effects of Low Doses of Melatonin Ingested in the Evening. *Clinical Pharmacology & Therapeutics.* 1995;57(5):552–558. doi:10.1016/0009-9236(95)90040-3

23 Meadows G. *The Sleep Book: How to Sleep Well Every Night.* Orion; 2014.

24 Trauer JM, Qian MY, Doyle JS, Rajaratnam SMW, Cunnington D. Cognitive Behavioral Therapy for Chronic Insomnia. *Annals of Internal Medicine*. 2015;163(3):191. doi:10.7326/M14-2841

25 Tang NKY, Lereya ST, Boulton H, Miller MA, Wolke D, Cappuccio FP. Nonpharmacological Treatments of Insomnia for Long-Term Painful Conditions: A Systematic Review and Meta-Analysis of Patient-Reported Outcomes in Randomized Controlled Trials. *Sleep*. 2015; 38(11):1751–1764. doi:10.5665/sleep.5158

26 Briñol P, Gascó M, Petty RE, Horcajo J. Treating Thoughts as Material Objects Can Increase or Decrease Their Impact on Evaluation. *Psychological Science*. 2013;24(1):41–47. doi:10.1177/0956797612449176

27 Hurt CS, Rixon L, Chaudhuri KR, Moss-Morris R, Samuel M, Brown RG. Identifying Barriers to Help-Seeking for Non-Motor Symptoms in People with Parkinson's Disease. *Journal of Health Psychology*. 2019;24(5):561–571. doi:10.1177/1359105316683239

28 Gollwitzer PM. Implementation Intentions: Strong Effects of Simple Plans. *American Psychologist*. 1999;54(7):493–503. doi:10.1037/0003-066X.54.7.493

29 Oettingen G, Hok G, Gollwitzer PM. Effective Self-Regulation of Goal Attainment. *International Journal of Educational Research*. 2000; 33(7–8):705–732. doi:10.1016/S0883-0355(00)00046-X

30 Aarts H, Dijksterhuis A, Midden C. To Plan or Not to Plan? Goal Achievement or Interrupting the Performance of Mundane Behaviors. *European Journal of Social Psychology*. 1999;29(8):971–979. doi:10.1002/(SICI)1099-0992(199912)29:8<971::AID-EJSP963>3.0.CO;2-A

31 Webb TL, Sheeran P. Mechanisms of Implementation Intention Effects: The Role of Goal Intentions, Self-Efficacy, and Accessibility of Plan Components. *British Journal of Social Psychology*. 2008;47(3):373–395. doi:10.1348/014466607X267010

32 Gollwitzer PM, Sheeran P. Implementation Intentions and Goal Achievement: A Meta-Analysis of Effects and Processes. *Advances in Experimental Social Psychology*. 2006;38:69–119. doi:10.1016/S0065-2601(06)38002-1

33 Prestwich A, Webb TL, Conner M. Using Theory to Develop and Test Interventions to Promote Changes in Health Behaviour: Evidence, Issues, and Recommendations. *Current Opinion in Psychology*. 2015;5:1–5. doi:10.1016/j.copsyc.2015.02.011

34 Maher JP, Conroy DE. Habit Strength Moderates the Effects of Daily Action Planning Prompts on Physical Activity But Not Sedentary Behavior. *Journal of Sport and Exercise Psychology*. 2015;37(1):97–107. doi:10.1123/jsep.2014-0258

35 Prestwich A, Kellar I. How Can the Impact of Implementation Intentions as a Behaviour Change Intervention Be Improved? *Revue Europeenne de Psychologie Appliquee*. 2014;64(1):35–41. doi:10.1016/j.erap.2010.03.003

36 van Osch L, Beenackers M, Reubsaet A, Lechner L, Candel M, de Vries H. Action Planning as Predictor of Health Protective and Health Risk Behavior: An Investigation of Fruit and Snack Consumption. *International Journal of Behavioral Nutrition and Physical Activity.* 2009;6(1):69. doi:10.1186/1479-5868-6-69

Chapter 5

Cultivating psychological skills

This will never work. You probably thought this at least once while reading this book, right? But you wouldn't be at Chapter 5 if you had given up all hope, would you? Have you ever heard the expression, whether you think you can or you think you can't, you're right? Science says this is true.

So far, we've identified the landscape of the condition with your specific symptoms, we've dug deep to define your personal values and we've formed goals that align with these values. Those values will keep you motivated along the journey and your goals will keep you focused on the big picture of the kind – life that you would like to lead. We looked at how emotions and thoughts can have an effect on the body. We worked through some strategies to cope with stress and minimise its impact on your physical and mental health. In the preceding chapter we took a closer look at the most common symptoms and I discussed how you can make a plan to manage the symptoms that are most troublesome to you. Now it is time to build up some psychological skills that will help your plans come into fruition and make lasting changes. Later in the book we will focus on behaviours, how to tame our impulses and form habits and how to communicate more effectively with loved ones and health professionals.

In this chapter I will talk about foundation psychological skills, skills that will help your plans fall into place. Think of it like the first domino you flick that creates a beautiful cascade. Except in this case, things aren't falling down, they are building up. A great example of a foundation psychological skill is self-efficacy. Believing in yourself will establish the frame of mind that will persevere and adapt, and problem solve to achieve your goals. As the 1st century poet Virgil put it: "They are able who think they are able".

If you only take one thing away from this chapter, it is the belief that you can do it. You must believe that you can manage your symptoms in a way that doesn't take over your life and you can enrich your life with things that are most valuable to you. If you don't believe, then you won't do it. I'm rooting for you, but you have to root for yourself. You just need to believe.

Losing previous roles and groups to which you used to belong can reduce how much you believe in your skills to cope and manage various situations. You lose the direct and indirect feedback you were getting from other people. Doing less stuff and being exposed to fewer experiences means you are less likely to develop and enjoy experiences that offer a sense of achievement. This can lead to you losing faith in your skills and capabilities. Not believing in your skills can make you put in less effort towards your goals, including managing your condition. You might persevere less and avoid tasks more.

We are more likely to do things if we believe we can. To develop this belief in our skills, or self-efficacy as psychologists call it, we need performance outcomes.[1] Past successes will influence whether you believe you are able to succeed. Successes like finding a good system to help you consistently take your medication, reading the leaflet that the doctor gave you and following the advice can make you realise that you have taken positive actions towards your health in the past and you can still do it now.

Take a moment now to think of all your successes in managing your health since you have been diagnosed. Better yet, write those successes down. Make it a habit to record your small or big wins. This will build your confidence in your ability to achieve the goals you set.

Another way to boost your belief in yourself is by setting realistic goals and appropriate timelines to achieve your goals. I'm not talking about lowering the bar so much that achieving your goals can come easily without much effort and difficulty. This will have the opposite effect on your belief in your skills. If goals are too easy to achieve, you won't have opportunities to practice perseverance, which is an important factor of success. Therefore, set goals that are slightly challenging but achievable.

Another way to boost your belief in yourself is identifying and studying role models. If you see someone like yourself achieving something similar to what you want to achieve, it will be easier for you to believe that you can do it. You can take this one step further and start imagining yourself doing the things you want to do. Think of every step of the way and then enact what you have imagined. Finally, your overall psychological state will have an effect on how much you believe in your skills. If you are discouraged, frustrated, or dejected, then you will be distracted and less likely to succeed. To boost your mood, you can revisit Chapter 3 on how to manage difficult emotions and stress (pp 55–80).

Seize control of your thoughts

Our minds are thought-producing machines. Most of these thoughts are noise; sometimes they are useful but when we want to solve a problem or think through an issue, thought production becomes a more conscious activity. For better or worse most of the thoughts we produce each day are just noise, things that are not relevant, lyrics from songs, phrases our parents used to say since we were very little, plans about things we should or shouldn't do, ideas of what we will do in the future or replays of past discussions. These thoughts are transient, they come and go; some of the thoughts are heavier and stickier and stay in our mind for longer while others are lighter and smaller and tend to be rather flitting.

"There is no point planning fun activities as my symptoms are so unpredictable. I never know how I'm going to feel in the next few days". "There is absolutely nothing I can do to help me with my pain". "It's so embarrassing going out for dinner, everyone is looking at me and my clumsy hands". All of these statements are lies we tell ourselves but regardless of how accurate these thoughts are, they create the same impact on our emotional well-being. The truth is far less harsh – making plans is always an option to give us a rough idea of how we want things to go and yes, there are plenty of things you can do about your pain, to prevent it from overtaking your life.

The following compelling thoughts, also known as thought distortions, can have an overwhelming effect on how we experience things. It will be helpful to understand them better in order to control them.

All or nothing thinking: you classify things as falling into only one of two categories. Example: I forgot to take my medication today. I will never be able to remember to take my medication on time.

Mind reading: You predict what others will think. Example: people will think I'm helpless if I ask for help with cutting my food when we're out.

Unhelpful rules: You adhere to strict rules that mess with your progress. Example: "I must carry on working late, even when I'm feeling ill".

Justification: You link two unrelated ideas to justify a decision. Example: "I don't need to think of other people's problems since my problems are more serious".

Delusional thinking: You convince yourself of something you don't really believe to justify a decision. "It's OK to skip my follow-up appointment with the neurologist".

Exaggerated thinking: you make a situation into something bigger than it is. Example: "I didn't manage to complete my physiotherapy exercises, my rehabilitation plan is ruined".

Thoughts are mental events that can have a huge impact on the way we feel emotionally and physically and on what we choose to do. Of course, the degree of this effect exists on a continuum and is determined by the context around the content. But generally speaking, negative thoughts will lead to low mood and with a long-term condition, negative thoughts are more likely to be present. Feeling low does not mean that you are going to develop depression. We all experience low mood, but it's important to learn how to reduce the amount of negative mood we experience to help us feel better in the long run.

The power of our thoughts is not a new one. Epictetus, the Greek philosopher, believed that people are disturbed not by things but by the views that they take of them. Similarly, Shakespeare had Hamlet declare that "there is nothing either good or bad but thinking makes it so". More recently Gandhi declared: "the man is a product of his thoughts, what he thinks, he becomes".

It is important for us to remember that uncontrollable events generate automatic (but changeable) thoughts, which generate feelings. Just like we can change our blood sugar levels and heart health by changing our diet and behaviour, we can change our thoughts by how we relate to events in our lives. And just like events, thoughts, ideas and feelings are changeable and imperma-nent. One moment they are upon us and the next moment some-thing else is in their place. Thoughts and images provide us with an indication of what is going on deeper in our mind at that very moment. By becoming aware of the thoughts that pass through our minds, we can become aware of the core beliefs we hold about a situation or event. With awareness comes understanding. With understanding comes the ability to make a healthier response to the situations we face.

All thoughts are only passing mental events. Just like other events in life, they happen and pass. Thoughts are not facts about us, the world in which we live, or the experiences that we have, but the result of many influences. For example, when we hear a bird we might have the thought, "that bird is making a beautiful sound" or "that bird is making an irritating sound". In either case, it is the same sound. It differs only in our thoughts about it. In other words, thoughts can be inaccurate, they can change, and they do not define us. They are interpretations that reflect what is happening in the world. Our mood influences what we think about a situation.

The idea that our thoughts or how we perceive a situation can drive our emotions is one of the main foundations of Cognitive Behavioural Therapy (CBT). CBT aims to help people deal with difficult emotions by changing their thought patterns. In CBT you question your thoughts and if they are not accurate or helpful you change them. Similarly, in Acceptance Commitment Therapy the thoughts are targeted but instead of trying to change them, people are encouraged to acknowledge them and let them be without over-indulging them. The different approaches suit different people but the key for both psychological approaches is to learn different ways to relate to your thoughts.

After a thought pops into your mind and before you react, take a breath or maybe a few breaths. Taking breathing space should always be the first step when dealing with a thought. With breathing comes an awareness that allows for a greater choice about how to respond. We have several choices. We can watch the thoughts come and go with awareness and without feeling that we have to follow them. Or we can view thoughts as mental events instead of facts and decide whether they are true or not. Once we assess the thoughts, we can choose which thoughts to act on and which to let pass by. Just remember, you have a choice. Paying careful attention gives us a different perspective of our problems so that the thoughts can, in turn, become less stressful for us.

Awareness of thought distortions and pessimistic thought patterns can help us experience fewer downward mood spirals. For every thought, we have choices of what to believe about them or what we can do (if anything) to change things. And if there is nothing you can do about a thought, could you let it be? Make space

for it and while it is around don't over-identify with it, don't feed
it with more negative thoughts. This will help you have a less emotionally charged experience and it might also help you let go of
these feelings and thoughts more easily.

Experiment with positive thinking

A lot of people with long-term conditions that I talk to frequently
tell me that they try to be positive to cope with the condition or
that being positive is all they need to do to cope. When I ask further
to really get to the essence of how they are positive and how can
they make themselves feel positive in bad days, little comes forward.
What they usually say is 'oh, I just think positively, I don't dwell on
the negatives'. People couldn't put their finger on something more
specific. I wanted the specifics, so I looked at the available scientific
evidence.

There does seem to be a power to positive thinking. It is not as
simple and direct a process as believing in something and making it
so. But believing that the future holds good things in store clearly
has an effect on the way we relate to many aspects of life.

Research from a variety of sources suggests that optimists cope in
more adaptive ways than do pessimists.[2] Optimists are more likely
than pessimists to take direct action to solve their problems, are more
prepared to deal with potential future issues and are more focused in
their efforts to solve any problem. Optimists are more likely to accept
the reality of the stressful situations they encounter. They seem intent
on growing personally from negative experiences and trying to make
the best of any situation. In contrast, pessimists are more likely than
optimists to react to stressful events by trying to avoid dealing with
problems and to quit trying when difficulties arise.

Researchers from the University of Miami asked women who
were dealing with breast cancer about their distress and coping
reactions before surgery, 10 days after surgery, 3 months after surgery, 6 months after surgery and a year after surgery.[3] Throughout this period, women who reported more optimism also reported
more acceptance of the situation and efforts to make the best of it.
The more optimism the women reported the less vulnerable they
seemed to be to distress.

But how can you become more optimistic if that doesn't come
naturally to you? Training matters when it comes to how we learn
and what we remember. It is enough to have trained your mind for a

particular reaction, for example towards the positive and away from the negative, for that reaction to take place in reality. If you have trained your mind to find the silver lining in things, faced with the next challenge you will be able to find some positive aspects of it. The Dalai Lama said that happiness is not something ready-made – It comes from your own actions. I take the Dalai Lama's words as a timely reminder of the need to train ourselves mentally for emotionally charged moments. It's easy to forget how quickly our minds grasp onto familiar pathways when given little time to think or when otherwise pressured. But it's up to us to determine what those pathways will be.

In research at Columbia, the neuroscientist Kevin Ochsner[4,5] has shown that teaching people to think of stimuli in different ways – to reframe them in positive terms when the initial response is negative, or in a less emotional way when the initial response is emotionally 'hot' – changes how they experience and react to the stimulus. You can train people to better regulate their emotions, and the training seems to have lasting effects.

Spending time with others is also important when it comes to training our minds on a more positive way of thinking. A lot of the participants in our study[6] talked about how their partners helped them when their coping strategies became more inflexible or they got caught up in doing certain things in a certain way that had become unhelpful. It is also helpful to plan activities with family and friends regularly. Go on. Take a diary and pencil in some dates and times to meet with people. It always helps with positive thinking to have things to look forward to.

Being optimistic is associated with our explanatory styles – the techniques we use to explain events. Martin Seligman, an American psychologist and promoter of positive psychology, describes 3 ways people can train their minds to make them more psychologically successful and less prone to depression: training people to change their explanatory styles

- from internal to external (from "I caused all bad events" to "Bad events aren't my fault"),
- from global to specific ("This is one narrow thing rather than a massive indication that something is wrong with my life"), and
- from permanent to impermanent ("At this moment, I feel sad" instead of "I will always feel sad").

The way you explain what caused past events will influence your expectations for controlling future events. Pessimism is a tendency to attribute negative outcomes to causes that are stable, global and internal. For example, "I did not understand what the doctor said about the treatment plan, because I am not intelligent". Optimism is the tendency to attribute negative events to causes that are unstable, specific and external. For example, I did not understand what the doctor said about the treatment plan, because the room was very noisy and I couldn't hear her very well.[7] An optimistic explanatory style is associated with higher levels of motivation, achievement and physical well-being and lower levels of depressive symptoms.[8]

A similar concept very closely related to optimism is the locus of control. Locus of control is a concept developed by the American psychologist Julian Rotter in the 50s and it is still being examined and researched. Locus of control is the degree to which people believe that they have control over the outcome of events in their lives, as opposed to external forces beyond their control. People with a strong external locus of control tend to praise or blame external factors such as their fate or the medical team whereas people with internal locus of control will attribute their success or failure on their skills or efforts. A more internal locus is tied to perceiving less stress and performing better. Additionally changing your locus from external to internal leads to positive changes in your psychological well-being and subsequently how well you will manage your symptoms.

The feeling of control is an essential element of happiness – a better predictor of happiness than, say, income. Having a feeling of autonomy, of being able to choose what happens in your life or how you spent your time, is crucial.

Christopher

> Christopher was a project manager in a tech company and he liked directing other people, coming up with streamlining processes and problem solving. After the onset of his condition he could no longer stay in that job, since it also involved a lot of travelling. He got involved with a youth charity, created a board to monitor the activities of the charity and a board to promote its activities. He used his previous job skills and felt responsible for a team of people but under different conditions". In his charity work he only had to travel to meet with his committee every couple of weeks and he kept up with developments mainly via email, something which he could manage, and the flexibility worked for him.

Finding ways to increase the control you feel you have over your life will help you think about things in a more positive light. Like Christopher, to feel more in control over a situation reframes how you see a situation and helps you find creative solutions to achieve what you want.

The cognitive skills that underpin happiness can be learned over time. Thought distortions commonly pop into our mind. The key is to recognise them for what they are and not let them highjack what we want to do and who we want to be. There are different ways to train yourself in positive thinking by directly re-adjusting your thoughts as they occur.

You can start by reframing a negative thought in a more positive light, seeing the silver lining in things. You have to attend a lot of appointments in the hospital but there is a lovely café just outside the hospital and you can spend some time there reading a book after the appointments. You can also reframe a negative thought by reminding yourself that this is a specific narrow issue. You had a setback with your disability allowance claims, you have to produce more documents but that doesn't mean it's a lost cause. You can also look for a different explanation for your experiences. You tripped over and fell. You are not clumsy, it was a very busy road and no one was looking where they were going.

You can also try to prevent negative thoughts popping into your mind in the first place: being with others, not trying to second guess what others say about us, getting some distance from our thoughts and seeing them for what they are, passing events and accepting things as they are, so we at least not fuelling the negative thought patterns.

We are all humans. We all make mistakes and a lot of the things that happen to us are not really our fault and we haven't caused them in any way. At the same time, no matter the problem, find an aspect that you can have control over. So even though we might not necessarily have control over what is happening we will have more control over how we respond and how we cope with what is happening.

Self-compassion

Self-compassion is taking an understanding and non-judgmental attitude towards yourself and being aware that your experience is not unique to you, but part of common human experience. We do things and feel things because we are humans, not because something is fundamentally wrong with us. You lost your patience and spoke abruptly to your spouse? Sure, it happens, we've all been there. You hit the snooze button one too many times and now everyone is late for school and work. You try not to do it again tomorrow but maybe you were too tired today. Humans get tired and demotivated sometimes. Self-compassion also means directing care, kindness and compassion towards yourself. OK, the cake is not the most photogenic but it tastes really nice and you put a lot of effort researching recipes, buying ingredients and making this cake. So, well done you. You did well!

If that sounds like naval-gazing and a bit self-indulgent, I hear you. Self-compassion sounds fluffy and lofty. At this point you might be rolling your eyes and turning the page but if you are still here, please, indulge me and carry on reading. I won't talk about unicorns and rainbows and visualising abundance. I'll talk about being kind. Imagine having a friend who is having a hard time, and who comes to you crying telling you her problem. Would you tell her to pull herself together? Would you tell her to stop being stupid/dramatic/overreacting? Now imagine seeing someone in crutches on the street losing his balance and falling, wouldn't you help him to stand and ask him if he's OK, rather than shout at him at how clumsy he is? In the same way you show kindness and concern for friends and strangers, you can show this kindness to yourself.

Viewed in one light, the reactions to highly self-compassionate people could also be interpreted as indifference, a refusal to accept responsibility (an avoidant or escape-oriented response), or as passivity (which could also be viewed as avoidance). However, self-criticism is probably more likely than self-compassion to lead people to avoid dealing with problems and to repress painful feelings. Research clearly shows that people who are self-compassionate are more likely to accept responsibility for their mistakes and failures than those who are less self-compassionate.[9] Treating themselves kindly despite their problems and failures allows people who are high in self-compassion to accept responsibility and to move on rather than getting caught up in defensiveness or denial. Given that self-compassionate people are less judgemental and more likely to forgive their own faults and inadequacies, they have less of a need to deny their failures and shortcomings. In fact, people who are high in self-compassion take greater responsibility for their failures and make needed changes while maintaining a loving, caring and patient

approach towards themselves. Being compassionate towards yourself instils a protective environment where it is safe to acknowledge
your inadequacies and seek ways to improve. Self-compassion
implies wanting the best for oneself, and this desire naturally leads
to positive self-changes.

Self-compassion is one of those foundation psychological skills
that will provide the basis of more psychological benefits. It can start
a positive psychological well-being domino effect. The most obvious
psychological benefit is decreased depression. German researchers
asked 2,404 people from the general public about self-compassion
and depressive symptoms and found that self-compassion has
the potential to buffer self-coldness related to depression[10] indicating that fostering self-caring, kindness and forgiving attitudes
towards oneself can have beneficial effects on psychological well-
being. People who are kinder and gentler towards themselves con-
strue negative events in less dire terms than people that are less
self-compassionate.

Self-compassion can also lead to proactive coping, in other words
using forethought and planning before problems arise. For example, making healthier food choices and exercising to avoid exac-
erbating your condition. Or looking into car modifications' costs
and options, before you need to modify your car just in case this
becomes a necessity.

These proactive steps have to come from a self-compassionate
place. You want to take care of your future self, you want to give
a present to the future you. You are not being proactive to please
others or because you don't like your current self. For example,
women who were high in self-compassion were motivated by their
personal values rather than any other outward reason, and their reasons for exercising were not related to ego concerns.[11] Another study
looked at how self-compassion was related to how women coped
after eating personally forbidden food.[12] Typically, highly restrictive eaters overeat after they break their diet, but in this study,
highly restrictive eaters who were led to be self-compassionate did
not overeat.

A lot of us in our quest for self-improvement and higher achievements lose our ability to be kind to ourselves. Paul Gilbert, the
founder of Compassion-Focused Therapy, calls this phenomenon
self-improving self-criticism. Self-improvers criticise themselves for
not being better than they are. They usually think that they are
not performing, or not achieving much, that they could do better.

These thoughts might be automatic, but they suck your energy like vampires and contribute to your fatigue. They bring you down and demotivate you.

Acknowledging these thoughts without fighting them is the first step. Treating yourself with care and respect is the second. When you are feeling down or demotivated, try to think what you would have said to a close friend of yours. Probably, you wouldn't have told your friend, when they were feeling down, that they have to try harder and that they are a failure. You would have encouraged them, maybe told them that they need to give themselves a break, maybe you would have invited them over for a cup of tea and some cake. The more you practice kindness towards yourself the better you become and soon the self-critical thoughts will be replaced with more compassionate ones.

If you want to see if you are high or low in self-compassion, next time something negative or stressful happens try to notice your imme-diate automatic thoughts. What sort of things do you tend to tell yourself? If things like "why do these things always happen to me?" and "I'm such a loser" tend to pop into your mind you are probably less self-compassionate. Further, if you have these sorts of thoughts, it is common to generalise these negative events to opinions about your-self and to think that you differ from other people in a negative way.

Being kind to yourself can manifest as taking time to spend on things you really enjoy or in engaging in positive self-talk that is encouraging and forgiving. Being self-compassionate also involves recognising that our experiences, no matter how painful, are part of the common human condition. When people fail, experience loss or rejection, are humiliated, or confront other negative events, they often feel that their experience is personal and unique when in real-ity, everyone experiences problems and suffering.

Realising that you are not alone in the experience reduces feel-ings of isolation and enhances our ability to cope with challenges. Being self-compassionate entails taking a balanced perspective of one's situation so that one is not carried away with emotion. When we face trials and tribulations, it's very easy to be carried away and dwell on the negativity of the situation and wallow in our emo-tions. In contrast, when we maintain perspective in the face of stress and approach the situation with a non-judgemental attitude we can cope more successfully.

Although little research has evaluated the relationship between self-compassion and proactive coping, self-compassion could play an important role in this process. People who cope proactively begin to prepare themselves in advance for possible distressing situations in the future. Therefore, one would presume that when stressors arise, self-compassionate people are more prepared to deal with their effects.

Putting it simply, being self-compassionate is being kind to yourself when it comes to your thoughts and your actions. The first step towards becoming more self-compassionate is catching any self-critical thoughts that pop into your mind. Acknowledge them but then let them go without getting in any sort of debate with them. We're not trying to eliminate thoughts; we try to give them less power. The next step is making a conscious effort to give yourself small pep talks throughout the day. Pat yourself on the back for every small win, every time you put effort towards something important to you, every time you show courage when it would have been so easy to stay quiet and do nothing. And when things don't go your way or you behave in ways that you didn't intend to, remind yourself that this is part of human nature, nothing personal. This non-judgemental stance will give you a more objective perspective of the situation, that consequently will lead to better ways of coping with difficult situations.

Build your 'uncertainty tolerance'

Everything in life is uncertain; we never know whether a bus will hit us on our way to work tomorrow or whether we will live into our hundreds, we don't know whether we will have the job we have today or something will happen and we will lose it unexpectedly. But having a long-term condition makes this uncertainty even worse. Things become even more fluid than they ever were.

When living with a long-term condition you might experience uncertainties around the identity of the condition and what it entails, its treatments, the way to navigate the health system and what factors contribute to the course of the condition.[13] Undoubtedly, concerns about whether, when, and how symptoms will progress are central to the experience of many long-term conditions.

High levels of symptoms such as pain are associated with uncertainty when you don't know how to manage them.[14] In breast cancer symptoms like fatigue and arm problems that can come and go can create uncertainty around recurrence of the condition.[15] In acute heart failure difficulty being aware of physical symptoms and determining their meaning is related to greater uncertainty.[16] Inability to determine the cause of the condition can also induce uncertainty.[17]

Uncertainty is not only limited to health-related issues since it spills into other areas of life. For example, employed patients may wonder about their ability to maintain a career and their financial stability; patients with children may wonder about their ability to satisfactorily participate in parenting and more broadly patients may worry about how the disease will affect their identity and quality of life. Families report that the presence of uncertainty disrupts family routines.

Uncertainty tolerance is a foundation psychological skill that provides the basis of other positive psychological outcomes. In fact, an increase in uncertainty tolerance can lead to clinical improvement across a variety of mental health diagnoses[18] whereas inability to tolerate uncertainty leads to worry[19] and rumination.[20] Intolerance of uncertainty has also been found to have an effect on the physical course of long-term conditions. For example, in Parkinson's disease uncertainty intolerance has been found to be related to motor fluctuations, anxiety and distress.[21]

Successfully coping with uncertainty is central to psychological well-being. The brain is a problem-solving machine and it needs to predict problems that may or may not happen and find solutions. When solutions are not readily available this will trigger uncomfortable emotions with the view to urge the brain to come up with solutions to various problems. When we have a long-term condition that puts the brain in overdrive the brain tries to help out – but it is not always helping. In other words, worrying about the uncertain future makes you believe that you ought to have more control and certainty in life. In reality, has your worrying made anything more certain or predictable? Does worrying really change the outcome of what will happen?

Some people, in order to minimise uncertainty, are willing to accept facts that are unfavourable to them; other people will seek out information to verify their preconceptions and beliefs.[22] Be mindful of these tendencies to avoid falling in the traps of quickly accepting things as facts or being biased towards the information you are getting so that you have some answers.

James,[23] an American philosopher and psychologist, argued that people try to simplify their experiences, but that any simplification that occurs is associated with a more fundamental search for certainty. An overly simplified worldview would be so crudely textured that it would be functionally meaningless and would therefore not provide subjective certainty.[24] As I said earlier in this book, you can't stop receiving stress from your environment, and if you do, you will end up living in a vacuum, but you can learn different ways to respond to it. Similarly, trying to eradicate uncertainty won't work.

Another way to manage uncertainty is to avoid thoughts about the future. Avoidance may at times be helpful. Choosing not to focus on the future of the condition, as it is not here at present, might be helpful. However, not planning for your future because you don't want to think about it can backfire and can result in more stress in the long run.

Other responses beyond avoidance may also be concerning, such as responding to uncertainty with hopelessness. For example, you may feel as if you are in a futile battle with your long-term condition. In this case, you might believe that no opportunities are worth pursuing. Unfortunately, many people in my research interviews have discussed their dreams or things they wanted to pursue but also felt there was no point pursuing those dreams due to their condition. People with a long-term condition who have difficulties tolerating the uncertainty and choose avoidance and hopelessness also report increased worry, threat perception, health-related anxiety and depression.[25, 26]

So, what are the best ways to increase your uncertainty tolerance? First of all, see if there is any way to minimise the uncertainty. Gain as much information about the condition as you feel comfortable with, use multiple reliable sources of information, take an active self-advocating role when it comes to interactions with health care professionals and confront negative or stigmatising behaviour.[27]

At a second level let's consider the situations that cause you to feel uncertain but are amenable to problem solving such as a current difficult relationship with someone from your health care team or being unable to drive. According to an article published in *Cognitive Therapy and Research* to improve your uncertainty tolerance, first, if you worry a lot about many things, try to stay focused on the problem situation. Try to identify all key elements of the problem situation while not paying undue attention to minor details related to the situation. Once the key elements have been identified, try to proceed solving the problem (see coping with stress p 67) even if you are not absolutely certain of its outcome beforehand. Seek a middle ground between trying to avoid the problem situation and attempting to gather excessive amounts of information about the situation, both of which delay problem solving and prolong worry.

Gathering appropriate information and problem solving cannot relieve all issues that cause uncertainty. For some situations problem solving doesn't cut it. For example, you might have a condition in which you know your symptoms will eventually progress but when and how is completely out of everyone's control.

When you feel uncertain, give yourself time to process what is happening. Seek out family members and friends that can help you come to terms with uncertainty. By discussing your worries with them, they can help you see uncertainty as part of a big picture and not as something that is threatening. Discussing your worries with your health care team can also help you acknowledge the natural existence of uncertainty so you don't end up seeing uncertainty as an anomaly that needs to be removed.

Uncertainty is a state with no emotions attached. It's the position where outcome cannot be predicted. The realisation that uncertainty is an inescapable part of reality can feel liberating in a world where no one can have a sure or final answer. We can control some things in life, but we cannot control everything. And the more comfortable we get with that thought the more space and energy we give to our brain to direct things we want to do with our lives. Uncertainty may be a time of flux that will eventually lead towards a new, higher order, a more complex orientation towards life.[28] Accepting uncertainty can help you develop a new ability to focus on multiple alternatives, choices and possibilities and to re-evaluate what is important in life situations.

Feelings of uncertainty are a common experience for all humans but they are likely to increase when you are facing a long-term condition. Feelings of uncertainty are associated with stress, anxiety, depression and worry for people with long-term conditions.

Being unable to manage your feelings of uncertainty or coping by ignoring situations (avoidance) or giving up trying (hopelessness) will eventually lead to increased psychological distress. Skilful management of the uncertainty feelings is a foundation psychological skill that will enable other positive psychological outcomes.

Sometimes feelings of uncertainty can easily be relieved by gathering more information about your situation and proactively trying to solve potential issues. However, a lot of the times, uncertainty cannot be relieved as easily. When uncertainty is a fact of unknown elements of the condition and there are no practical/tangible steps you can take to relieve the feeling of uncertainty, try to switch the way you perceive uncertainty. Accepting uncertainty and seeing it as just a fact of life and nothing to be afraid of you lessen any harmful events. You can go a step further and see how this uncertainty is opening up new opportunities, for example to connect more meaningfully with people you love, to prioritise in a different way in life. Discussing your feelings of uncertainty with family, friends and your health care team can help you broaden your perspective and see uncertainty in a different light.

Cultivating new psychological skills

In our work with people with Multiple Sclerosis we have found that people who seemed happier with how they manage their condition were the ones who could adapt their behaviour and coping style to different situations as the condition progressed[6]. In a deliberate or instinctual way, they persisted or changed their behaviour in line with a new situation or their goals and values. In this chapter I discussed some useful psychological skills that you can master to help not only with issues that are present but also potential future challenges.

In this chapter we covered some basic psychological skills that have been linked with increased psychological well-being. Skills is the key word here. I am not talking about personality predispositions that we have or don't have. I am talking about qualities that we can practice and with practice we can make progress.

For me and based on vast scientific evidence the skill that is the most important on improving psychological well-being and better symptom management is what psychologists call self-efficacy: the confidence that you have the skills required to achieve your goals.

The bad news is that having a long-term condition means that you potentially socialise less with others, thus you receive less validation from others and you expose yourself to fewer experiences and opportunities that will give you a sense of achievement. All these can chip away your confidence in your abilities.

The good news is that there are ways to build your confidence back up again. Think about your past successes, write them down and be vigilant to current wins, no matter how small. Keep a log of all your current and past successes as a reminder that you can do it. You got this. You also need to be setting realistic goals within achievable timeframes. Not setting yourself up for failure but at the same time not setting the bar too low and losing the opportunity to practice perseverance and grit. Surrounding yourself with people in a similar situation or with similar goals who are trying and achieving their goals can serve as a constant reminder that what you want to do can be done. It can also help to use some visualisation techniques imagining the path you want to follow to achieve your goals. Imagining the steps and what you need to do will prepare you and get you into action. Finally, look after your overall mood and psychological health. It is much easier to feel confident about our skills to succeed when we feel happier and more optimistic we feel.

We are thinking beings. The body responds to the type of thoughts the brain produces, and emotions will also be impacted. Thought distortions and helpless thought patterns can lead to a downward mood spiral. Recognising these thoughts when they pop into your mind is the first and most important step to managing them. The second step is not letting them take control of what you do and how you feel. Take a breath and a step back from the thought. Don't feed the thought with more negative thoughts. Examine it for the moment, label it and see whether it is something you need to address or something that is best to let go.

To proactively take control over our thoughts, we should not only try to recognise the thoughts as they come into the mind and minimise their impact. We can also train ourselves to produce more positive and less judgmental thoughts. Believing that the future has good things in store has an effect on how we cope with stressful situations by encouraging better future planning and applying the right effort to solve problems.

Actively trying to find the silver lining in situations, will help the brain develop pathways that will make it easier to think in a positive way. You can also train yourself on how you explain situations that haven't gone as expected. Think about all the different reasons that contributed to what happened. Are there any things that were outside of your control? Anything that you could change in the future?

Another psychological skill worth pursuing that leads to positive psychological outcomes is self-compassion. Self-compassion means treating yourself with kindness. As with positive thinking the more you practice self-kindness the better you get at it. Practice telling yourself kind and encouraging things and reminding yourself that your experiences, no matter how painful, are part of the common human condition. Dwelling on emotion can make you lose perspective. Talking to friends and family or people with the same condition as you can help you to regain perspective and realise that your situation is not as unique as you thought. Also spending time doing things that you enjoy and value is another demonstration of self-kindness. And when you have small or big wins in the day or enjoy something, take a moment to acknowledge it to make sure it registers.

Finally, tolerating uncertainty related to illness issues or life in general (work, childcare etc) has been associated with a domino effect of positive psychological outcomes like reducing depression and anxiety and improving quality of life. See if there are any ways that you can minimise the uncertainty by gaining more information about the condition or other issue that is worrying you. As you are gathering information try to remain objective and unbiased. Don't be quick to accept any sort of information, especially from unreliable sources, just to regain some certainty or seek out information that will confirm your preconceptions. By gaining more information you can identify areas of the issue that you can have some control over and you can make a plan on how to resolve things. But avoid falling into the trap of gathering excessive information that will only overwhelm you. Finally, see if it is possible to change the way you see uncertainty. Being not certain is a piece of a bigger picture. It is a state with no emotions attached, just a position where outcome cannot be predicted.

Believing that you can achieve your self-management goals, gaining more understanding of your thoughts and practising positive thinking and uncertainty tolerance could all support you psychologically and provide a solid base for you to build a self-management system that works for you.

Bibliography

1 Bandura A. Self-Efficacy: Toward a Unifying Theory of Behavioral Change. *Psychological Review*. 1977;84(2):191–215. doi:10.1037/0033-295X.84.2.191

2 Scheier MF, Carver CS. Effects of Optimism on Psychological and Physical Well-Being: Theoretical Overview and Empirical Update.

Cognitive Therapy and Research. 1992;16(2):201–228. doi:10.1007/BF01173489

3 Carver CS, Pozo-Kaderman C, Harris SD, et al. Optimism versus Pessimism Predicts the Quality of Women's Adjustment to Early Stage Breast Cancer. *Cancer*. 1994;73(4):1213–1220. doi:10.1002/1097-0142(19940215)73:4<1213::aid-cncr2820730415>3.0.co;2-q

4 Ochsner KN, Gross JJ. The Cognitive Control of Emotion. *Trends in Cognitive Sciences*. 2005;9(5):242–249. doi:10.1016/j.tics.2005.03.010

5 Ochsner KN, Bunge SA, Gross JJ, Gabrieli JDE. Rethinking Feelings: An fMRI Study of the Cognitive Regulation of Emotion. *Journal of Cognitive Neuroscience*. 2002;14(8):1215–1229. doi:10.1162/089892902760807212

6 Bogosian A, Morgan M, Bishop FL, Day F, Moss-Morris R. Adjustment Modes in the Trajectory of Progressive Multiple Sclerosis: A Qualitative Study and Conceptual Model. *Psychology & Health*. 2017;32(3):343–360. doi:10.1080/08870446.2016.1268691

7 Scheier MF, Carver CS. On the Power of Positive Thinking: The Benefits of Being Optimistic. *Current Directions in Psychological Science*. 1993;2(1):26–30. doi:10.1111/1467-8721.ep10770572

8 Buchanan GM, Seligman MEP. *Explanatory Style*. L. Erlbaum; 1995.

9 Leary MR, Tate EB, Adams CE, Allen AB, Hancock J. Self-Compassion and Reactions to Unpleasant Self-Relevant Events: The Implications of Treating Oneself Kindly. *Journal of Personality and Social Psychology*. 2007;92(5):887–904. doi:10.1037/0022-3514.92.5.887

10 Körner A, Coroiu A, Copeland L, et al. The Role of Self-Compassion in Buffering Symptoms of Depression in the General Population. *PLoS One*. 2015;10(10). doi:10.1371/journal.pone.0136598

11 Magnus, MRC. *Does Self-Compassion Matter Beyond Self-Esteem with Women's Self-Determined Motives to Exercise and Exercise Outcomes?*; 2007.

12 Adams CE, Leary MR. Promoting Self-Compassionate Attitudes toward Eating among Restrictive and Guilty Eaters. *Journal of Social and Clinical Psychology*. 2007;26(10):1120–1144. doi:10.1521/jscp.2007.26.10.1120

13 Mishel MH. Reconceptualization of the Uncertainty in Illness Theory. *Image: The Journal of Nursing Scholarship*. 1990;22(4):256–262. doi:10.1111/j.1547-5069.1990.tb00225.x

14 Johnson LM, Zautra AJ, Davis MC. The Role of Illness Uncertainty on Coping with Fibromyalgia Symptoms. *Health Psychology*. 2006;25(6):696–703. doi:10.1037/0278-6133.25.6.696

15 Wonghongkul T, Dechaprom N, Phumivichuvate L, Losawatkul S. Uncertainty Appraisal Coping and Quality of Life in Breast Cancer Survivors. *Cancer Nursing*. 2006;29(3):250–257. doi:10.1097/00002820-200605000-00014

16 Jurgens CY. Somatic Awareness, Uncertainty, and Delay in Care-Seeking in Acute Heart Failure. *Research in Nursing and Health*. 2006; 29(2):74–86. doi:10.1002/nur.20118

17 Sharkey T. The Effects of Uncertainty in Families with Children Who Are Chronically Ill. *Home Healthcare Nurse*. 1995;13(4):37–42. doi:10. 1097/00004045-199507000-00006

18 Talkovsky AM, Norton PJ. Intolerance of Uncertainty and Transdiagnostic Group Cognitive Behavioral Therapy for Anxiety. *Journal of Anxiety Disorders*. 2016;41:108–114. doi:10.1016/j.janxdis.2016.05.002

19 Buhr K, Dugas MJ. Investigating the Construct Validity of Intolerance of Uncertainty and Its Unique Relationship with Worry. *Journal of Anxiety Disorders*. 2006;20(2):222–236. doi:10.1016/j.janxdis.2004.12.004

20 Julien CL, Rimes KA, Brown RG. Rumination and Behavioural Factors in Parkinson's Disease Depression. *Journal of Psychosomatic Research*. 2016;82:48–53. doi:10.1016/j.jpsychores.2016.01.008

21 Brown RG, Fernie BA. Metacognitions, Anxiety, and Distress Related to Motor Fluctuations in Parkinson's Disease. *Journal of Psychosomatic Research*. 2015;78(2):143–148. doi:10.1016/j.jpsychores.2014.09.021

22 Rokeach M. *The Open and Closed Mind: Investigations into the Nature of Belief Systems and Personality Systems*. Martino Fine Books; 2015.

23 James W. *Principles of Psychology*. Volumes 1 and 2. CreateSpace Independent Publishing Platform; Combined edition; 1890.

24 Hogg MA. From Uncertainty to Extremism. *Current Directions in Psychological Science*. 2014;23(5):338–342. doi:10.1177/0963721414540168

25 McEvoy PM, Mahoney AEJ. Achieving Certainty about the Structure of Intolerance of Uncertainty in a Treatment-Seeking Sample with Anxiety and Depression. *Journal of Anxiety Disorder*. 2011;25(1):112–122. doi:10.1016/j.janxdis.2010.08.010

26 Boswell JF, Thompson-Hollands J, Farchione TJ, Barlow DH. Intolerance of Uncertainty: A Common Factor in the Treatment of Emotional Disorders. *Journal of Clinical Psychology*. 2013;69(6):630–645. doi:10.1002/jclp.21965

27 *Applied Interpersonal Communication Matters: Family, Health, & Community Relations (Language as Social Action)*. Peter Lang Inc., International Academic Publishers; 2006.

28 Antonovsky A. *Unraveling the Mystery of Health: How People Manage Stress and Stay Well*. Jossey-Bass; 1987.

Chapter 6

Lifestyle changes

Developing healthy behaviours will strengthen your body and help you deal with your current condition. Healthy behaviours might help prevent you from getting any additional health condition that will complicate matters a lot more. Behaviours like quitting smoking, losing some extra pounds, doing some moderate exercise, reducing salt in your diet, reducing alcohol and eating more fruits and vegetables all help to keep a stronger body. These behaviours are activities that can be directly or indirectly measurable. Having the intention to eat three fruits a day is not a behaviour. Wanting to lose weight is a goal but not a behaviour, but walking in the park every morning is a measurable activity linked to your intentions and goals.

What is healthy behaviour and how much of it is actually needed is a complicated issue. What is classified as a healthy behaviour changes over time as medical knowledge advances, and cultural and resources vary. In the '50s children were encouraged to eat the fat off the meat and in the USA in 1919 the dietary advice promoted a healthy meal of bread, milk and cookies.

Your healthy behaviours are also somewhat independent; for example, you might floss your teeth but at the same time have a lot of sugar in your diet. You might be exercising but still drink to excess. In this chapter, I'll talk about how to change behaviours so hopefully you can pick up some tricks to help you with behaviours and habits you want to change.

And we also know that healthy behaviours are not stable over time. There might be a period in your life that you have the time to go for a run and drink a fruit and vegetable smoothie in the morning, but you have children or a much longer commute and you only have time for a black coffee and a cereal bar on the go. Here, I will discuss further how to keep that motivation going.

Our personal values motivate our health behaviours and habits. And sometimes there might be a conflict in these values. We do value our health and want to go to sleep early to keep the body healthy and rested. At the same time, we also value spending time with loved ones and staying up late with your partner is also high on your values list. If while reading the following chapter you notice that conflicting values are an issue for you, choose one of the two or more values to focus on. That one value will guide you through the behaviour change process.

Adherence to medication

For any treatment to be effective, the very first step is to adhere to the given medication. Medication non-adherence for patients with long-term conditions is extremely common, affecting as many as 40% to 50% of people who are prescribed medications for management of long-term conditions such as diabetes or hypertension.[1] Non-adherence is a prevalent and very complex problem. The solution can be quite easy and straightforward or more complex.

Let's look at the most straightforward solutions to help you keep up with your medication. Then we will look at more complex barriers and issues that might be at play.

Become medication smart. It's up to you to take or not to take the medicines you have been prescribed. Before you make any conscious decisions about not taking the medication, read about them and ask your doctor. What are the active ingredients of the drug? How and when it is best to take them? What are the potential side effects? In which cases do you need to alert your doctor, e.g. when specific side effects appear? An essential piece of information to consider before making any decision is how the medication benefits your condition and when to expect to see benefits or what will happen with your condition if you don't take the medication.

If you decide that you would like to take the medication, but you find it challenging to remember to take the drug, a quick and easy way to remember to take your medication is by using prompts. The prompts can be post-it notes at high visibility areas in the house (above the kettle?). Or you might want to bundle medicine taking with a well-established routine that happens at the intervals you need to take your medication. For example, you need to take your medicine once a day. You always without fail have to eat breakfast each morning, so what about merging taking your medication with having breakfast? Finding a system to monitor the dosage or whether you took the medication that day is also essential. For example, you might want to buy the 7-day pillboxes so you have a visual reminder and monitoring device at once. Or you can simply place a tick on the wall calendar once you take your medication.

You might be thinking, how come I can't stick to my regime even though I know how necessary the medication is and how serious the condition can get without them? You are not alone; how severe the illness is has nothing to do with your ability to stick to a medication regime.[2] Many reasons can explain this, so don't be too hard on yourself. Let's look at some common factors that are in play to see which resonate with you.

The most common and the most manageable issue to address is lack of understanding of the instructions, of what it is needed to be done. How often does the medication need to be taken, will you be able to open the bottle, know how to inject? If something is not 100% clear to you, ask for clarification. Doctors and nurses are happy to explain, and you will be helping future patients as doctors and nurses will become aware of the lack of clarity. Researchers have found that one of the most effective ways to improve adherence to medication is the 'teach-back' method. When a health professional is explaining to you the what, how, when, and what ifs of taking medications, you then explain back what you have understood from their explanations.

Another reason why you might find it challenging to stick to the new medications might have to do with retrospective memory. Retrospective memory is the memory of people, events and words encountered or experienced in the past. It is easy to forget the details of the medication plan. It might help if you write down what needs to be done or ask your doctor/nurse to illustrate examples of the plan for you to facilitate understanding and memory.

Prospective memory, remembering to perform a planned action or recall a planned intention in the future, is another issue that might be in play here. Retrieval of the information needed, when needed, can be improved by event-based retrieval or time-based retrieval. In English, it means that you remember to take your medications as you have planned when you associate taking your medication with a specific time (time-based retrieval). For example, it's 3 p.m., meaning it's the time that you always take your medication. Also, you can associate taking your medication with a specific event (event-based retrieval). For example, finishing your dinner means you take your medication.

There are also other more complex reasons you might be finding it difficult to take your medication. Maybe taking medications reminds you of the illness, and you are not yet in a place that you can accept this aspect of yourself. Not taking medication protects you from feeling like a 'patient' and enables you to carry on as usual. But in the longer term, what is it costing you? Think back to your values. What really matters to you, and how consistent are your actions with your values?

Maybe you don't think that the drugs help, and it makes no difference whether or not you are taking them. Perhaps it's challenging to adapt your lifestyle, you don't have the time, you have other more pressing priorities, you are too tired. Maybe the side effects of the medication feel worse than any potential benefit. Or you feel comparatively optimistic; you don't feel you will get sicker if you don't adhere to the medication. It is important to take a few moments to reflect on what you think is really behind you not taking the medication. See if you can discuss some of these issues with your health care team. For example, it might be worth learning how important it actually is to adhere to the medication and what happens if you don't.

It is useful to discuss with your health care provider your concerns about potential adverse effects of the medication and any doubts about the necessity of the medication. They might be able to provide you with new information to consider before making any choices about your health care plan.

Many patients receiving regular medication who have not experienced adverse effects are still worried about possible problems in the future. These often arise from the belief that regular use can lead to dependence, or that the medication will accumulate within the body and lead to long-term effects. These issues are the social representations of medicine as being harmful and over-used. For example, worries that corticosteroid inhalers prescribed for asthma will result in weight gain or that regular use of pain medication now will make it less effective in the future.

All of these thoughts might not be happening in an apparently deliberate way but might underpin your trouble with adhering to the medical treatment. For example, in some situations non-adherence could be the result of a deliberate strategy to minimise harm by taking less medication. It has been shown that individuals who do not perceive their medication to be important are more likely to forget to take it. The impact of perceptions of treatment on adherence is also influenced by beliefs about adherence, such as the importance of strict adherence to achieve the desired outcome. Again, talking to your health care team will help you get some clarity on those issues.

There is also maintenance treatment – the medication you have to take to retain benefits. In these cases, the medication does not make you feel better. Missing doses may not immediately make you feel worse, which makes it extra hard to adhere to such medications.[3,4] However, in long-term conditions, maintenance treatment is very common. If you have any concerns about your medication talk to your health care provider; they will welcome the feedback and they might have the same concerns as you. They won't take this as doubting their skills but as an opportunity to work with you more collaboratively. You have a common goal of finding the best type of treatment regime, one that is the most convenient for you with the fewest side effects.

Adhering to the healthcare regime will lead to fewer consequences of the condition. If taking the medication helps you perform daily activities, it's worth reflecting on your beliefs and feelings on your treatment plan. Articulate any concerns to your health care provider.

Physical activity

Regular exercise can assist the treatment of many health conditions, including secondary prevention of coronary heart disease, stroke rehabilitation, treatment for heart failure and prevention of diabetes as well as improving symptoms for back pain, chronic kidney disease and osteoarthritis.[5] Exercise improves blood pressure, blood sugar levels and blood fat levels like cholesterol. It helps you maintain a good weight, which takes the stress off weight-bearing joints. Being physically active is also part of keeping bones healthy and treating osteoporosis. Regular exercise can also help prevent blood clots. Indeed, this is one of the reasons physical activity can be of particular benefit to people with heart and vascular diseases. Studies with people with heart disease show that exercise improves the health of their heart and their quality of life. Regular exercise has been shown to help people with chronic lung disease to improve their endurance and reduce the trips they make to A&E. Many people with leg pain resulting from poor regulation can walk further and more comfortably with a regular exercise programme. Regular exercise improves levels of strength, energy and self-confidence and lessens feelings of stress, anxiety and depression. Regular exercise can also help you sleep better and relax and feel happier. I won't go on, you get the picture. If you already have formed a habit of exercising regularly, well done! You can skip this section. If you would like to increase your current levels of physical activity, carry on.

The first step is to build up your self-efficacy, the confidence that you can do it. Research evidence shows us two ways to build up self-efficacy, when it comes to exercising. You can build this confidence through past successes in physical activity or other areas in your life and through watching others achieve their physical activity goals.[6] Think of the things you have already accomplished; you did it before, you can do it again. Also, if you know someone with a regular exercise regime, ask them what systems they put in place to exercise regularly.

The good news is that it doesn't take hours of painful, sweat-soaking exercise to achieve health benefits. Even short periods of moderate physical activity can improve health and fitness, reduce disease risk and boost mood. Being active also helps you to feel more in control of your life and less at the mercy of your health condition. According to the NHS website, for general health adults are advised to do at least 150 minutes a week of aerobic activity – in other words, 30 minutes of aerobic activity five days a week, and two or more days a week of strength exercises.

It is not about hitting those targets, the important thing is to do something active that you enjoy every day. If you want to just make a start, buy a cheap pedometer or download a free app for your phone and set a goal of specific steps you want to do a day. Tracking your steps will motivate you to keep going. I have recently bought a very basic pedometer. It's surprising how effective it is. Sometimes I will pace up and down the room when getting my baby to sleep or when talking on the phone, just to see the little medal appear on my pedometer that I reached my steps target. Research has also shown that having goals and monitoring a simple physical activity like walking can increase your physical levels[7].

If your vision and/or mobility is limited, you can adjust your workout goals. You can try different physical activities like swimming, sitting exercises, wheelchair workouts or using a rowing machine adapted for wheelchair use. If you are a wheelchair user, you can use the traditional pedometers adjusted to the wheelchair setting or buy a wheelchair-specific accelerometer. Or you can use other data to track to keep you motivated, for example, time spent on physical activity or difficulty level.

Charities organise local physical activity groups so you can have a look at their websites to see what is available near to you. These community classes are sometimes offered free of charge or require small contributions. If you don't like group activities, you can join a gym and get a personal trainer for a few sessions to work out a routine that fits you. There is an abundance of yoga and Pilates studios and some specialise in people with physical challenges, although these may be expensive. Even gardening has been found to improve mood state for people attending a cardiac rehabilitation program.[7]

House chores are also a form of physical activity, if you only think of them this way. Researchers at Harvard University[8] recruited room attendants from eight different hotels. When you are a room attendant, you're on your feet all day. You're pushing a vacuum cleaner back and forth, wiping down surfaces, sweeping, lifting trash cans, carrying piles of sheets and towels – all of this adds up to a lot of exercise. But most room attendants don't think of it as exercise. It's their job.

The researchers split the room attendants they recruited into two groups. In one group, the room attendants were presented information about the calories they burnt when they perform various tasks of their job, which were quite a lot. The other group was not provided any information about how their work could be described as exercise. For both groups, the researchers took various measurements related to health and fitness, e.g. blood pressure, height, weight, body fat percentage, waist and hip size. The researchers returned in a month and collected the same health and fitness measurements. The overall result from these measures is that the two groups didn't change their eating or exercise habits. However, the general fitness levels of the group who had received info about the calorie expenditure had dropped their weight, percentage of body fat and blood pressure.

And it dropped without any change in behaviour. All that changed was the way they thought about their jobs. They thought of their job as exercise. Thinking about your everyday physical activities as exercise enables your body to get more out of it.

Yet, if you want to add more exercise in your days and you want to make exercise a lifelong habit, find joy in whatever you choose to do. Maybe listen to a compelling audiobook while you are exercising that can make you come back to the gym just to carry on listening to the story. Or find a type of exercise that sounds fun to you. I have heard people talking about boxing and dance classes they attend in their local recreation centre. Involving others also helps you to keep on track of your physical activity. Could you organise a small group of close friends to go swimming with you for three mornings a week and then you can have breakfast all together?

Make sure you get advice from a professional about the right type of physical activity for you. If your fitness levels, strength and muscle mass have been reduced due to your condition, you run a higher risk of getting an injury.

Time is a persistent barrier for people taking up exercise or sticking with it. We all have the same amount of time; we just use it differently. It's a matter of priorities. If you have time to watch television, you have time to exercise. Exercise doesn't take a lot of time. Just 15 minutes a day is a good start, and it's much better than nothing. You may be able to fit exercise into your day; for example, why not watch television while pedalling a stationary bicycle? If you take three 10-minute walks three times a day, you have 30 minutes of daily exercise.

Also feeling tired can prevent you from exercising the way you have planned or even prevent you from starting. When you are unfit or depressed, you can feel exhausted. You have to break out of the 'very tired' cycle. There are different types of fatigue, and sometimes we feel mentally fatigue and sometimes it's physical fatigue. When mentally fatigued, even though we don't feel like exercise, our body can actually handle activity and in fact can help energise us. Try an experiment: next time you are tired, take a short walk, just for five minutes, or even two minutes will do. You may be surprised that this gives you energy. As you get fitter, you will recognise the difference between feeling listless and feeling physically tired. The more you do, the easier it becomes to see change.

It may be that you are unable to do a vigorous or strenuous exercise programme. Still, you can usually find ways to be more active. Remember, you can start with exercise for only one minute, several times a day. Better fitness will help you cope with your illness and prevent further problems.

If you don't use a wheelchair a lot, but you'd need to use it when exercising, the lack of confidence in your skills using a wheelchair might be another barrier. Again, starting small can help here. What is the minimum you feel confident starting off with? Start from there and slowly build up your skills and confidence.

Another common barrier preventing people from taking on exercise is the fear of falling. If that's the case, make sure to exercise somewhere where you are unlikely to fall. This means good lighting, well-maintained parking and pavements, handrails and uncluttered floors.

Smoking

Quitting smoking is one of the best gifts you can give to your body. Excess risk of heart attack caused by smoking reduces by 50% within 12 months of quitting smoking. Quitting smoking returns the rate of decline in lung function to the normal age-related decline. Within five years of quitting, stroke risk is reduced to that of a non-smoker. Within ten years, the risk of lung cancer falls to about half that of a smoker and the risk of cancer of the mouth, throat, esophagus, bladder, cervix and pancreas decreases.[9]

Smokers who stop show reduced levels of stress and mood disorder than those who continue.[10] They also report higher levels of happiness and life satisfaction than those who continue.[11] This suggests that smoking may harm mental health, though other explanations cannot be ruled out, based on the current evidence.

According to a review published in the *Chronic Obstructive Pulmonary Disease* journal[12] the best advice for helping smokers to quit includes setting clear and realistic goals, monitoring your progress and adjusting things along the way to help you reach your goal. Focus on your new non-smoker identity and the reasons you decided to quit smoking in the first place.

When stressed or when the environment makes it more difficult for you to stick to your resolution to quit, make it easier for yourself to resist the urge to smoke. First, avoid your triggers. For example, avoid alcoholic drinks or coffees if you have associated them with smoking. Or avoid visiting your smoker friends' house; instead meet them in a public place so smoking is not an option. Second, create barriers. For example, make it extra hard for you to access cigarettes, tobacco, lighters and ashtrays. Tame your urges. Think of your urges like waves – they emerge, get bigger, but always crash on the shore and disappear. Don't react to them, ride them and watch them go. We'll talk more about habits later on, but for now, a quick tip is to try to create competing habits. This means habits that are antithetical to smoking, things like going for a long walk in the morning or roasting vegetables with olive oil and herbs when you feel stressed.

To increase your chances of success, get a professional to help you along the way. Stop smoking advisers are available all over the UK. You can join a local group that meets once a week or have one-to-one support. You usually meet for a few weeks while working towards a quit date. You can find your nearest Stop Smoking Service on the NHS Smokefree website or call the Smokefree National Helpline on 0300 123 1044 to speak to an adviser.

You can also consider nicotine replacement aids. Nicotine replacement therapy can help reduce the severity of withdrawal symptoms and reduce the harmful desires, urges and smoking satisfaction.[13] Nicotine replacement products address the need to smoke arising from 'nicotine hunger'. Medications that have been shown to substantially improve smokers' chances of achieving long-term abstinence are nicotine replacement therapies, bupropion, varenicline and nortriptyline substantially improve smokers' chances to achieving long-term abstinence.[14,15,16] The nicotine replacement aids work by reducing the need to smoke and impulses that are driven by certain cues. For example, your friend lighting a cigarette will prompt you almost automatically to also lit a cigarette. Bupropion and varenicline also reduce the satisfaction from the cigarette smoked if a lapse occurs. Your pharmacist or your stop smoking adviser can give you more advice on the appropriate nicotine replacement therapy.

Following is an example of the plan you can put in place when you decide to quit smoking.

Pre-quit

Identify the reasons for quitting. Think about your big picture, your big WHY, the personal value that drives you. This will keep you motivated through all the highs and lows, the ebbs and surges.

Then plan how you are going to achieve your goal. What resources you will need? Maybe you need someone to be your cheerleader and sounding board. Perhaps you need to purchase nicotine replacement products. Or maybe you need to buy trainers to start going for a morning walk or run. Think about the ways you will make it easier for yourself to quit, so you don't have to rely on self-control so much. Change things in your environment. If you have your cigarettes next to your coffee machine and reach for them when you wait for your coffee to brew, you can replace them with a fancy notepad and pen to write your to-do list for the day. Maybe you need to rearrange that meeting you have with your friend in a different location that you know will be smoke-free.

You also need to set your personal goal and decide what your success will look like and how to measure success. Form a clear 'not a puff' rule after your definite quit day. You can also measure your success not only on cigarettes not smoked but also on building up your new competing habit or resisting going out for a drink, which is a trigger for you.

Next, get an appointment with a stop smoking advisor to help you fine-tune your plan and also give you advice on the best nicotine replacement product for you. It is a good idea to start using nicotine replacement products a couple of weeks before quitting partially to extinguish associations between smoking and nicotine reward.[17] With nicotine from the nicotine replacement products competing with nicotine from cigarettes for the receptors, there will be a partial dissociation between the act of smoking and its effects in the brain. The stop smoking advisor will also help you boost your belief that you can do it and keep you motivated.

Quit day

In your planned first smoke-free day you need to observe how things are going for you and identify any barriers that make staying smoke-free more difficult. When and under what circumstances do you find the temptation to smoke more irresistible?

The first day you also need to use any support from family and friends that you can get. You need people to encourage you and help you remove any triggers, for example, avoid smoking in front of you.

Finally, you will need to start using your nicotine replacement products, if you haven't done so already.

Post-quit

You also need to have some tricks up your sleeves that will help you remain smoke-free in the long run. Very commonly, the momentary urge to smoke exceeds the decision not to, and a lapse occurs. What usually happens is not that people decide to go back to smoking permanently but merely to suspend the rule. Oh, it's just this one cigarette. And the truth is one cigarette, one lapse does not matter in the long run. But how often is it really only one cigarette? Think about each choice you make of smoking or not, not as an isolated incident, but as a choice that would be repeated. Remember that you're not trying to be perfect. The lapses may be part of your journey. But if you're trying to change habits and build new ones, try to focus on building the habits you want to repeat.

Carry on seeing your stop smoking advisor or a health psychologist to support you to sustain your motivation not to smoke. Professionals can also help you develop a strong identity that excludes smoking and manage urges to smoke. They can also help you optimise use of medication after the quit point, gauge progress and assess whether treatment is still required.[18,19,20]

Increasing your motivation

Motivation is commonly thought of as the 'reasons' for doing something. This implies it is a mostly conscious and deliberate activity, which is true, but that is not entirely true. Motivation is better defined as everything that makes a person do what they do – anything that energises and directs their behaviour. The motivational state is a moment-by-moment property which is shaped by different systems of influence, physiological, impulses and inhibitions, motives, beliefs and identity.

Inside everyone there is a voice of reason that says things like "I need to go to sleep early to be able to have a good rest" and an impulsive voice, who says things like "no, let's watch another *Breaking Bad* episode because this is more pleasurable now". The voice of reason represents conscious processes, has decided what is good and bad, forms conscious intentions and makes decisions and plans. The impulsive voice represents unconscious processes and is driven by emotions, desires and habits.

Your motivation goes through highs and lows. One day you spring out of bed, take your medicine, have a healthy smoothie while massaging your feet the way the physiotherapist shows you and another day you want to pull the covers over your head unable to face the day. Adding to that, a lot of long-term conditions come with fluctuating symptoms, your motivation highs and lows can be even more pronounced. But not all is lost, there are a few things you can do to keep your motivation more stable.

Research has shown that four factors influence motivation: identity, beliefs about change, habits and emotions. I talked about managing emotions in the previous chapter. But let's talk about all the other factors in turn here.

Identity

People are more likely to do things if they are consistent with how they like to see themselves. For example, parents might give up smoking because they believe that being 'a good parent' is inconsistent with exposing their child to harm. We do things that make us feel good and avoid things that make us feel bad.

The social psychologist Claude Steele first proposed the theory of self-affirmation. A major insight of the theory involves the notion that although people try to maintain specific self-images (such as 'being a good parent' or 'being a good citizen'), that is not their primary motivation. Rather we are motivated to maintain global self-integrity, a general perception of our goodness, virtue and efficacy.

We have a fundamental motivation to maintain self-integrity, a perception of ourselves as good, virtuous and able to predict and control important outcomes. We also view ourselves as able to control outcomes that we objectively cannot. And we take excessive credit for success while denying responsibility for failure.

Psychologists have found that when we experience a threat to our sense of self, we reject information that causes that threat because we want to protect positive self-feelings. We want to feel that we are good, competent, capable of free choice and capable of controlling important outcomes.[21] This tendency can have detrimental effects to our health or we can use it to our advantage.

For example, if we receive messages about alcohol being bad for our health and we are sensible/capable people, we could stop listening to any info about the matter thinking: "why would a sensible person like me engage in an activity that is bad for me?" Therefore, we block all the relevant messages that make us feel less sensible.

What we tend to forget or ignore is that us being good and capable and sensible and able to control our life does not depend on a solo behaviour. We are still amazing even when we drink a glass of wine after work, even when we binge drink at our cousin's wedding. Hey, we are human, we are amazing humans. The self-integrity system is also flexible.[22] Global self-integrity can be maintained by affirming other domains. In this way, global self-integrity remains intact, despite the presence of the threatening information. Take for example alcohol consumption. Researchers from the University of Manchester[23] found that people reduced the amount of alcohol they consumed when they made a plan to start thinking about the things that are important to them every time they felt threatened and anxious (e.g. when some label or some person told them about the dangers of alcohol consumption). In a similar study[24] participants were asked to pour a safe level of wine into glasses. One group of people had standard wine bottles whereas the other group had wine glasses with a label that encouraged the participants to think about things that were important to them when feeling threatened. The researchers found no difference in amount of wine poured but the group with the reminder to think about valued things drank significantly less at the follow-up.

What all these mean in practice for you is that connecting to your personal values and thinking about who you want to be and what you want to stand for as a whole can lead to better choices for you, choices that align with things that are important to you and help you avoid doing things that you will later regret or make you feel worse. Having some not-so-perfect parts of your life does not detract from the fact that you are a good person.

Forming new habits

We all have good intentions to wake up early, eat healthy and not smoke or drink as much, but the intentions in of themselves do not propel us to action. In fact, research shows that the intention to do something predicts only around 20% of whether we will do it.[25] Intention is even less important when it comes to previously formed habits.[26] You also don't require any intention to act a certain way. So, let's skip the talk about our intentions to do things and talk about how we can do things. Habits are the kings of the action. They are initiated without awareness and require little to no effort.[27]

Having a long-term condition means that some of your habits need to be altered or that new habits need to be formed to enhance your health and your overall well-being. Your body is now dealing with a condition and it's trying its best to keep things going, so no need to make this job harder. For most conditions, a healthy balanced diet, moderate exercise, quitting smoking, reducing alcohol consumption, adhering to medication and check-up appointments all will help you keep on top of things. Also, having a long-term condition might mean that you have less energy or less time when you are pain-free and you would like to spend this time doing the things that make you feel fulfilled the most.

Habits are performed frequently because they are automatic responses to situational cues.[28] They are a learned sequence of acts that have been reinforced in the past by rewarding experiences and that are triggered by the environment to produce behaviour, largely outside conscious awareness. The three key aspects of habits are that they are outside of our awareness, they are beyond our control and are mentally efficient.

The strength of routines and habits help us to order the world and regard it as reliable; when you regard the world as reliable you don't have to think about it – you don't have to be alert. If you can trust your environment, then it becomes a foundation for more outgoing activities.

Habits are automatic responses, which means they do not require intention, they may be initiated outside of volitional control and require little or no effort.[27] To form a habit you need to repeat the behaviour frequently; when the habit is formed the behaviour is automatic.

Habits are cue-response associated.[29] In other words, we have certain cues that will trigger some behaviours; for example, you might automatically reach for the jar with the cookies when feeling lonely or light a cigarette when having a glass of wine. If those triggers are not encountered, the behaviour will not happen. Therefore, when the context of our lives changes, as it happens when diagnosed with a long-term condition, some of the previously formed habits might also change. Some of these changes might be welcomed, some of them not.

Habits are formed when a cue (for example the end of a meal) is associated with a response (e.g. eating chocolate) and this cue-response situation has been repeated over time. Where habit is strong, you don't need any time to review information and options and make decisions and what you intend to do will be overruled in favour of the habit. In fact, you will use very little time and energy to perform that behaviour that is a habit. For example, say your habit is to eat chocolate after dinner; if that habit is strong, it doesn't matter what you have decided. You may have all the good intentions to eat more fruits and cut down on chocolate. Also after dinner you are more likely to reach for chocolate rather than apples.

Our habits are relatively independent from one another. The habits are qualitatively different to each other; for example you can exercise but that doesn't prevent you from also consuming alcohol in excess.

And you might also have noticed from your own experience that 'good' and 'bad' (whatever good or bad means to you) habits are not stable over time. There might be a period of your life that you may exercise then you decide you prefer to stay in and watch endless episodes of *Friends*.

Another quality of habits that is good to mention here is that the habits are driven from different values. For example, you value your health but you also value spending time with your friends. Even though you have decided to cut down on alcohol you might go to the pub for a few pints with your friends. These two habits are motivated by different values that clash and one of them will take second place.

Now, let's put the theory into practice. To form a habit: 1. link this new behaviour to something that is already a well-established part of your routine, 2. Plan to repeat the behaviour for at least two months, or until it feels 'automatic'.

There is a common misconception that you need 21 days to form a habit. That came from a widely popular 1960 book called *Psycho-Cybernetics* by Dr Maxwell Maltz, a plastic surgeon who noticed his patients seemed to take about 21 days to get used to their new faces. However, a study published in the *European Journal of Social Psychology* shows that forming a habit varies from 18–254 days.[29] How long it will take depends on a few things.

The frequency: is it an hourly habit? A daily habit? A weekly habit? A monthly habit? An hourly habit will likely take much less 'time' to develop. If it's a monthly habit, it can't take any less than 2 months, since you need to repeat the behaviour to become a habit.

The effort: how soon you will form a habit also depends on the effort you put in. Practice makes progress. The more effort you put into planning, preparing and pursuing this new habit, the sooner you'll get there. Commit to doing the behaviour as consistently as possible.

Monitor, reinforce and re-evaluate the success as you progress with the forming of your habit. The gap between where you are now and where you want to be will determine how soon you will form the behaviour. Regularly monitoring how well you are doing with your new behaviour will keep you motivated and ensure that you apply the right kind of effort into creating a new habit. Naturally, the narrower the margin between your current habit and your new habit, the less time it will take to adopt that new habit – providing you are putting in the work.

To summarise, in order to form a habit, link the desired behaviour to something that is already a well-established part of your routine. Commit to doing the behaviour as consistently as possible, plan to repeat the behaviour for at least two months or until it feels 'automatic' and finally, monitor, reinforce and re-evaluate the success.

Start with one habit but don't stop there; once you have established a habit try forming another one. Forming multiple healthy habits can benefit you more and there is some evidence showing that mortality risk for those with four compared to zero health behaviours was equivalent to being 14 years younger.[30]

Changing habits

But how can you change some of the habits that don't serve you anymore and replace them with habits that will help you keep on top of things? How you change an already established behaviour? Habits are not formed or changed because you read compelling evidence about how healthy or unhealthy they are. Disruption of established habits requires conscious, self-directed effort. In plain English: to change a behaviour you have to plan for it. Habits get in the way of us changing what we do. Unfortunately, being motivated to do something and having the intention to create a new habit are not enough. They cannot carry you through to changing habits that don't align with your current values. You will need some heavy-lifting habit-disruption strategies in your back pocket.

To reverse an old habit that no longer serves you, you need a context dependent repetition. Recognise the cue that triggers your habit and either find a compelling alternative behaviour to compete with the established habit or if possible, change the cue.

How do you replace the habit you want to change? Let's go back to our example where you eat chocolate after dinner, and you want to stop doing that. First you have recognised the cue, i.e. having dinner, and then you work out how to behave differently in its presence, for example, you eat fruits after having dinner. In order to facilitate that behaviour you may want to restructure your personal environment, for example don't keep any chocolates in the house and have the fridge well stocked with fruits, or even have a fruit bowl featured always in the middle of the table for a reminder of your new behaviour and also for easier reach when dinner is done. By changing the environment when the cue is present (you finish your dinner), it will be easier to perform your new behaviour.

There are habits in which it might make more sense to eliminate the cue. Let's say you are in the habit of buying alcohol when you pass the corner shop on your way back from work. You could change your route so that the cue (the corner shop) does not appear to trigger your alcohol-buying behaviour.

Monitoring, reinforcement and re-evaluating the success is as important for changing a habit as it is for forming a habit. You can use positive reinforcement, AKA rewards. Reward yourself for performing your new habit. You don't want to use rewards all the time. In fact, that can decrease those desired behaviours, because we become less motivated by the rewards over time.

Ever get acknowledged by a doctor or a nurse for doing really well sticking with your treatment and coping with it all? It felt pretty good, right? If your doctor or nurse sings your praises for every pill you are taking, every health-check appointment you attend, every hour you spend working out, their praise would no longer mean anything. It'd no longer be rewarding. So, while we don't want to rely on rewards too much to change a habit, we do want to keep some in our back pockets. Rewards can be things, showing yourself a little love, doing something social, or investing in your health. The rewards can be tangible or they can be experiences.

Monitoring your progress and finding new ways to measure this progress is also important. Let's say losing some weight is one of your doctor's pieces of advice to ease the pain in your knees due to osteo-arthritis. If your goal is to lose weight and you measure your success using the scales it can be de-motivating when you reach a plateau and your weight doesn't seem to change. Progress can mean weight loss, but it can also mean a whole lot of other things. Though you might not be losing weight every day, you're making progress every single day.

To recap, habits are unlikely to respond to information alone. Disruption of established habits requires conscious self-directed effort, i.e. plans. Recognising the cue and working out how to behave differently in its presence is one way to break a habit. Planning to do a compelling alternative behaviour to compete with the established habit is another way to break habits. Finally, monitoring, reinforcement and re-evaluating success can help along the way.

Roadmap for changing behaviour

When it comes to changing behaviour, we all behave and see how others behave and have our own theories about how to change behaviour but they can be wrong. There is a science of behaviour change and this chapter was based on this method. It's not a magic bullet. To change a behaviour we need to understand it. Specifically, why are behaviours as they are? And what needs to change for the desired behaviour to occur? The same behaviour, e.g. not taking our medication, may be caused by many different factors. Successfully dealing with the behaviour (i.e. changing it) depends on having an accurate understanding of the causal factors.

To break a habit that no longer serves you, you need to break the behaviour chain. You don't just polish off a slice of cheesecake without thinking while watching TV. There is a subconscious process that controls every action you take. It's called the behaviour chain. Understanding your behaviour chain is the first step to breaking a habit. All behaviour chains have one thing in common: they start with a trigger.

Triggers come in many shapes and sizes. They can be environmental, biological, mental, emotional, or social. Imagine being at a party where hot sausage rolls, a huge variety of cheeses and a chocolate fountain are in display (environmental trigger). The hostess approaches you and asks you to try the cake she made – it is a new recipe and it took forever to make the cream fluffy and smooth (social trigger). You had a dispute with your partner, and very little sleep last night, you feel completely worn out (mental and emotional triggers).

Triggers will produce thoughts and feelings. Thoughts are your great friends but occasionally can be very unfriendly and say things to you like "You are at a party, have a good time", "your friend is so eager for you to try his cake, it's rude not to try", "You had a rough day, you deserve a cheese platter just to replenish all the calories you used up battling with sleep last night".

These thoughts lead to actions. Actions like reaching out your hand, snatching up the last mozzarella ball and tossing it into your mouth. Not only do actions have consequences, but there are

four distinct types of consequences: physical (body related), physiological (bodily function), psychological (thinking patterns) and emotional.
In our mozzarella example, the consequences would likely be:

- That was delicious (physiological).
- My stomach doesn't feel so good (physical).
- Wondering "why did I do that?" or "what's wrong with me?" (psychological).
- Feeling disappointed or guilty (emotional).

Mapping out your behaviour chain:

1   The trigger: _____

2   Thoughts and feelings: _____

3   Actions: _____

Mapping out your behaviour chain is the first step needed to break it. Now you know what to look for.
Changing your behaviour involves three deceptively straight forward steps, what I call the 3T approach. 1. Target, 2. Tracking and 3. Tweaking. The first step is to set your target, what you want to achieve. Define a specific SMART (Specific, Measurable, Achievable, Relevant, Timely) goal with an if-then rule (If I don't go out for a walk two days in a row, then I will call my friend to meet up and I will walk to her house). First, you visualise your goal. It can be something as simple as putting on clean clothes every morning to doing my physiotherapy exercises three times a week. Then, picture the steps. How you would choose the clothes to wear the next day, laying them out next to the bed and then waking up and slipping into them as soon as you open your eyes in the morning. Next, imagine anything that can get in the way. You had a bad night, you are planning to have another nap in a couple of hours, no one will be around the house to see you today. Then, craft a specific answer to any of those possible roadblocks, in the form of simple if-then statements; if I'm sleepy, I'll have a coffee while dressing up; if I'm worried that no one will see me anyway, I'll sit out in the balcony to have lunch. Create an implementation strategy to avoid obstacles and find payoffs. If it all

sounds just common sense, you are right. It is. And it also works. Don't take my word for it. Try it out.

Then find a way to monitor your progress towards this goal. You can do this by either setting up mini goals, setting deadlines, or by putting a cross on the days you performed the behaviour. Finally, you tweak your plans as you go along, regularly checking your progress against your goal and seeing if the goal or your methods for achieving this goal need adjusting.

You also need a good structure around your 3T method to support you along the way. Think about any prompts or changes you can make to your environment to make things easier for you. Things like placing your pills in a more visible place, decorating your kitchen counter with a basket full of fruit or buying non-alcoholic beverages that you enjoy having. You also need to sharpen up your problem-solving skills. Finally, set reminders for yourself to perform the behaviour. The reminders can be post-it notes dotted around your house, asking your partner or friend to remind you to keep on track when you lose motivation or stop performing the behaviour or it could be bundling the behaviour you want to adapt/change with something you enjoy doing and you do regularly, for example, drinking a glass of water when reading the news first thing in the morning or taking your pills while having your breakfast each morning.

Think about the behaviours you want to change within the context they are happening. Also consider the likelihood that you stick with that new behaviour. How easy is it to do? Does it cost a lot of money? Time? Will you like doing it? Any positive spillover effects? Every behaviour is within a network of behaviours within a person and every person is within a network of other people. Now write down all the behaviours that you are interested in changing to improve your health or to better manage your condition.

- e.g. Book an eye check appointment.
- Text a friend to go out for a walk.
- Look into chair yoga studios in my area.
- Go to my pharmacist to see what help I can get to quit smoking.

Pick one behaviour that you want to start with and think of what you want to do differently, when, where and how. And don't forget that behaviours are often dependent on or influenced by other behaviours, yours or other people's.

Bibliography

1 Kleinsinger F. The Unmet Challenge of Medication Nonadherence. *The Permanente Journal*. 2018;22. doi:10.7812/TPP/18-033

2 DiMatteo MR, Haskard KB, Williams SL. Health Beliefs, Disease Severity, and Patient Adherence: A Meta-Analysis. *Medical Care*. 2007; 45(6):521–528. doi:10.1097/MLR.0b013e318032937e

3 Horne R, Weinman J. Self-Regulation and Self-Management in Asthma: Exploring the Role of Illness Perceptions and Treatment Beliefs in Explaining Non-Adherence to Preventer Medication. *Psychology & Health*. 2002;17(1):17–32. doi:10.1080/08870440290001502

4 Halm EA, Mora P, Leventhal H. No Symptoms, No Asthma: The Acute Episodic Belief Is Associated with Poor Self-Management among Inner-City Adults with Persistent Asthma. *Chest*. 2006;129(3):573–580. doi:10.1378/chest.129.3.573

5 Hoffmann TC, Maher CG, Briffa T, et al. Prescribing Exercise Interventions for Patients with Chronic Conditions. *CMAJ: Canadian Medical Association*. 2016;188(7):510–518. doi:10.1503/cmaj.150684

6 Ashford S, Edmunds J, French DP. What Is the Best Way to Change Self-Efficacy to Promote Lifestyle and Recreational Physical Activity? A Systematic Review with Meta-Analysis. *British Journal of Health Psychology*. 2010;15(2):265–288. doi:10.1348/135910709X461752

7 Soga M, Gaston KJ, Yamaura Y. Gardening Is Beneficial for Health: A Meta-Analysis. *Preventive Medicine Reports*. 2017;5:92–99. doi: 10.1016/j.pmedr.2016.11.007

8 Crum AJ, Langer EJ. Mind-Set Matters: Exercise and the Placebo Effect. *Psychological Science*. 2007;18(2):165–171. doi:10.1111/j.1467-9280.2007.01867.x

9 WHO. Fact Sheet about Health Benefits of Smoking Cessation. *WHO*; 2013.

10 *Smoking and Mental Health*. RCP London. www.rcplondon.ac.uk/proj ects/outputs/smoking-and-mental-health. Accessed December 15, 2019.

11 Shahab L, West R. Differences in Happiness between Smokers, Ex-Smokers and Never Smokers: Cross-Sectional Findings from a National Household Survey. *Drug and Alcohol Dependence*. 2012;121(1–2):38–44. doi:10.1016/j.drugalcdep.2011.08.011

12 West R. The Multiple Facets of Cigarette Addiction and What They Mean for Encouraging and Helping Smokers to Stop. *COPD: Journal of Chronic Obstructive Pulmonary Disease*. 6;2009:277–283. doi:10. 1080/15412550903049181

13 West R, Baker CL, Cappelleri JC, Bushmakin AG. Effect of Varenicline and Bupropion SR on Craving, Nicotine Withdrawal Symptoms, and Rewarding Effects of Smoking during a Quit Attempt. *Psychopharmacology*. 2008;197(3):371–377. doi:10.1007/s00213-007-1041-3

14 Cahill K, Lindson-Hawley N, Thomas KH, Fanshawe TR, Lancaster T. Nicotine Receptor Partial Agonists for Smoking Cessation. *Cochrane Database of Systematic Reviews*. 2016(5). doi:10.1002/14651858. CD006103.pub7

15 Hughes JR, Stead LF, Hartmann-Boyce J, Cahill K, Lancaster T. Antidepressants for Smoking Cessation. *Cochrane Database of Systematic Reviews*. January 2014. doi:10.1002/14651858.CD000031.pub4

16 Stead LF, Perera R, Bullen C, et al. Nicotine Replacement Therapy for Smoking Cessation. *Cochrane Database of Systematic Reviews*. November 2012. doi:10.1002/14651858.CD000146.pub4

17 Shiffman S, Ferguson SG. Nicotine Patch Therapy Prior to Quitting Smoking: A Meta-Analysis. *Addiction*. 2008;103(4):557–563. doi:10.1111/j.1360-0443.2008.02138.x

18 Gwaltney CJ, Shiffman S, Balabanis MH, Paty JA. Dynamic Self-Efficacy and Outcome Expectancies: Prediction of Smoking Lapse and Relapse. *Journal of Abnormal Psychology*. 2005;114(4):661–675. doi:10.1037/0021-843X.114.4.661

19 West RJ, Hajek P, Belcher M. Severity of Withdrawal Symptoms as a Predictor of Outcome of an Attempt to Quit Smoking. *Psychological Medicine*. 1989;19(4):981–985. doi:10.1017/S0033291700005705

20 Shiffman S, Engberg JB, Paty JA, Perz WG, et al. A Day at a Time: Predicting Smoking Lapse from Daily Urge. *Journal of Abnormal Psychology*. 1997;106(1):104–116. doi:10.1037//0021-843x.106.1.104

21 Steele CM. The Psychology of Self-Affirmation: Sustaining the Integrity of the Self. *Advances in Experimental Social Psychology*. 1988;21(C):261–302. doi:10.1016/S0065-2601(08)60229-4

22 Sherman DK, Cohen GL. The Psychology of Self-Defense: Self-Affirmation Theory. *Advances in Experimental Social Psychology*. 2006;38:183–242. doi:10.1016/S0065-2601(06)38004-5

23 Armitage CJ, Arden MA. A Volitional Help Sheet to Reduce Alcohol Consumption in the General Population: A Field Experiment. *Prevention Science*. 2012;13(6):635–643. doi:10.1007/s11121-012-0291-4

24 Armitage CJ, Arden MA. Enhancing the Effectiveness of Alcohol Warning Labels with a Self-Affirming Implementation Intention. *Health Psychology*. 2016;35(10):1159–1163. doi:10.1037/hea0000376

25 Armitage CJ, Conner M. Efficacy of the Theory of Planned Behaviour: A Meta-Analytic Review. *British Journal of Social Psychology*. 2001;40(4):471–499. doi:10.1348/014466601164939

26 Norman P, Conner M. The Theory of Planned Behaviour and Binge Drinking: Assessing the Moderating Role of Past Behaviour within the

Theory of Planned Behaviour. *British Journal of Health Psychology.* 2006;11(1):55–70. doi:10.1348/135910705X43741

27 Bargh JA, Chen M, Burrows L. Automaticity of Social Behavior: Direct Effects of Trait Construct and Stereotype Activation on Action. *Journal of Personality and Social Psychology.* 1996;71(2):230–244. doi:10.1037/0022-3514.71.2.230

28 Verplanken B, Aarts H. Habit, Attitude, and Planned Behaviour: Is Habit an Empty Construct or an Interesting Case of Goal-Directed Automaticity? *European Review of Social Psychology.* 1999;10(1):101–134. doi:10.1080/14792779943000035

29 Lally P, Van Jaarsveld CHM, Potts HWW, Wardle J. How Are Habits Formed: Modelling Habit Formation in the Real World. *European Journal of Social Psychology.* 2010;40(6):998–1009. doi:10.1002/ejsp.674

30 Khaw K-T, Wareham N, Bingham S, Welch A, Luben R, Day N. Combined Impact of Health Behaviours and Mortality in Men and Women: The EPIC-Norfolk Prospective Population Study. Lopez A, ed. *PLoS Medicine* 2008;5(1):e12. doi:10.1371/journal.pmed.0050012

Chapter 7

You don't have to do it all on your own

Christina

Paul wants Christina to try harder and push herself. He keeps saying if you don't use it, you'll lose it. "He was married to a very independent self-sufficient woman, and he does not want to lose that". Christina thinks. Paul is tired of talking about MS all the time, and he wants to be supportive and help Christina to 'beat MS' and not give up. Christina feels under constant pressure to perform at a high level. She is afraid of asking for help and thinks that her relationship with Paul adds to her stress levels, and at times this stress has contributed to relapses. To avoid another relapse, she avoids contact or communication with her husband apart from the bare minimum that is necessary – house logistics and practicalities related to their children. Paul is efficient and rational. He's the best person to ask for help when she feels too tired to work out problems or make decisions, but she doesn't because she doesn't want him to see 'her weaknesses'.

The breakthrough came when the company Christina was working for was relocating to a different country, and she was asked to join the company with a promotion and pay rise. Christina initially did not want to discuss this with her husband, but when conversations began, she found herself loosening up and talking about all different issues she had suppressed over the years. Her husband was understanding and with his usual 'let's fix this' attitude made helpful suggestions and helped her sort out her conflicting thoughts not only about taking up the promotion but also how to find a better balance between taking care of her health while following her dreams. Paul was happy that he could help and felt that his opinions were valued. Christina realised that her husband was not pushing her and stressing her out of lack of understanding or because he wanted her to be a certain way; genuinely, it was how he thought he was helping her best.

Talking openly about what each wanted and was thinking and not accusing the other or defending their position or guessing what the other wants or thinks can lead to more meaningful relationships and happier lives.

The story of Christina might sound like a clear case of miscommunication but is not uncommon. And as with many things we are better able to spot faulty patterns of communication in others and be blind to such miscommunications in our own lives. And of course, the more people we interact with the higher the likelihood of misunderstandings, arguments and judgements.

Relationships require intentional effort. Steve Duck, in his book *Relating to others*[1] argues that if we put up with the occasional oppressive obligation that might happen once or twice in a lifetime, our everyday relationships offer abundant delights and benefits. They are real daily consequences of the need to *do* relationships. We are often required to coordinate two timetables, two sets of preferences and needs, or two sources of demands that are created by the uniting of the two otherwise independent beings into one relational entity. Of course, such accommodations have psychological consequences and are challenging to do, not merely pleasures of relating to others.

Long-term condition for many people means an increase in interaction with doctors and paramedics, hospital appointments, difficult discussions with family members, or increased dependency on other people. A long-term condition proliferates social interactions, from doctor visits to asking strangers for help with things, which naturally increases the chances of a conflict. Also, a long-term condition can contribute to changes in the roles in the family and force you to be more assertive than you usually would. Research shows a strong effect of negative social support on health. For example, people involved in serious conflicts with family or friends were more likely to develop a cold virus[2] and people who reported hostile marital interactions also had slower wound healing.[3] And unfortunately, these negative social interactions and conflicts have longer-lasting negative effect than positive social interactions.[4]

On the other hand, when the relationships are harmonious, they can buffer the adverse physiological effects of stress. Research also shows that people after being diagnosed with a long-term illness re-evaluate their priorities and decide to focus on and nurture relationships with family or friends. Therefore, those relationships are strengthened. There is an increasing body of evidence demonstrating the benefits of peer support and community groups in combating isolation and helping people sustain their knowledge, confidence and skills over time.[5]

Unlike an acute health event, a long-term condition is ongoing, which means that you will require a network of people over time. You will need a convoy of people who accompany you through life and provide varying degrees of emotional and practical support at different time points. No one person can provide you with all the support you need and satisfy all of your needs. Support needs will change throughout an illness and so will social network functionality and structure.

I said earlier that having a long-term condition means that you are the only one who can take charge in managing it. You are in charge, but you don't have to be alone in this journey.

Friends and family can be there to help. Maybe they don't know what to say, but you can assist them. Tell them what you need to hear and what help you need. Tell them that it is OK not to know what to say. Get them involved in the diagnosis but be mindful that whereas you might have come to terms with what is happening, they might not be ready yet. People have different timelines to respond to challenges and different ways. Ask them to respect your way, and you respect theirs. When it is time, you can discuss the things you need to help you cope.

Common problems in communication

"You just don't understand!" I'm pretty sure you've said that in despair before shutting down a conversation at some point since you have been diagnosed. We've all been there. This failure to communicate effectively can upset you which is the last thing you need when you have a long-term condition. When communication breaks down our symptoms may increase. Pain can get worse, blood glucose and blood pressure levels may rise, and there is an increased strain on the heart. Conflict and misunderstanding can make us irritable and interfere with our concentration. Poor communication is bad for our physical and mental health.

We often think of conversation as a contest if someone disagrees with us. Our minds are wired to think of ourselves as better-than-average in everyday situations, and when our thoughts are challenged, we naturally think of ourselves as right. All of these tendencies compel in us a view that talk is fundamentally simple and that if someone doesn't understand us, it must be their fault. But there is a great deal more to our talk than our surface assumptions suggest – to become better, we need to know more and blame less.

In the midst of a conflict, our body responds. For instance, we feel edgy, we fidget, our shoulders and neck tense up and our fingers clench into a fist. Our muscles are responding automatically to biochemical changes. Our individual awareness of and ability to talk about feelings varies significantly. Few people are conscious of the interaction between our feeling and thinking processes and their effect on the way we communicate with each other.

When emotions are running high, we're more likely to use language that implies blame, causing the other person to feel under attack as at once the other person is on the defensive and the barriers go up. The situation escalates from there, leading to anger, frustration and bad feelings.

Healthy communication is the cornerstone of relationships between spouses, partners, family members, friends, co-workers and members of your health care team.

Often when we communicate, we use indirect means. Instead of saying what we really want, we are abstract, or we expect the other person to know what we mean. Do not make assumptions regarding others because 'they should know': people are not mind readers. They won't know for sure unless you tell them. No one knows what we want to say, unless we express it clearly – it's that simple. This implies that we know what we want to express. If you are not sure what you want to express, do not rush. First, review the situation. Next, decide exactly what is bothering you. Then, ask yourself what you are feeling. For example, I feel embarrassed when my husband talks on my behalf when we are in public. This is a clear message that you can communicate and resolve a situation.

Accusing and judging can make people become defensive and our communication becomes especially difficult. Describe a specific situation and your observations should stick to the facts. Avoid words such as always and never. For example, instead of saying "you never help me with anything", try saying "Could you help me with the dishes tonight?"

Respecting the other, giving them space and time can help communication, but without forgetting ourselves and everything we want to express. Sometimes silence can say a lot, as well as a touch, an eye contact. Not everything can be expressed with words. Unfortunately, often the other person uses blame and then we blame the other person. In these cases, thoughtful communication can be helpful. Expressing our emotions, wants and needs focuses the discussion to us and gives room to others to speak for themselves. This way both sides can be freely expressed.

Communication is a two-way process. While you may feel uncomfortable about expressing your feelings or asking for help, the chances are that other people may also feel the same way. Why don't you lead the way and model open communication? You cannot change the way other people communicate. What you can do is change your way of communicating to make sure that you are understood.

To be more effective communicators, we have to become more emotionally intelligent. This concept was introduced in 1995 by Daniel Goleman in his book *Emotional Intelligence*.[6] The psychologist Reuven Bar-On defined emotional intelligence as "our ability to recognize, understand and use emotions to cope with ourselves, others and the environment". There are several important recurrent findings in the research into emotional intelligence: people who can read their own emotions and recognise their impact are likely to be good at reading others' emotional states. They also seem to be more aware of their overall strengths and limitations, which contributes to a sound sense of one's self-worth and capabilities. People who can manage their feeling reactions – who can keep their disruptive emotions and impulses under control, particularly in difficult situations – are seen as more trustworthy, honest and of high integrity.

Even a dispute or a fight can be freeing, as there are times that tension and bottled-up emotions need an exit. The sure thing is the more we keep them bottled up, they will come out with greater force. It would be best to express our wants and needs regularly and not keep things under the rug that will eventually come out with force and aggression towards the other.

Speaking honestly and directly may upset the other and cause anger. Can I handle this? Maybe the 'good child' that still exists in many of us wants to keep everyone happy. The 'good child' doesn't share their feelings and true thoughts or they say things in a very sweet and polite manner.

Express your feelings openly and honestly. Others cannot guess accurately what you are feeling. The chances are that they may be miles out. Bottling up your feelings, particularly anger, can sometimes lead to chronic stress. As we know, this can have an effect on our physical health. Try to always be honest with your feelings even when it may seem that you are being critical of someone else.

Further, for someone who doesn't express their needs it is very easy to adopt the role of the 'victim' since no one understands their wants and needs. Who else though is responsible if not us to express what we keep inside?

There are people who don't listen, and others who don't talk; in each case none of them communicates but remains alone in their own world. There are people with an aggressive attitude who keep fighting and others who are a calming force in tensions and don't like confrontations.

Based on our experiences, each of us has developed a unique way to communicate. And this can change when we realise and feel how we want to communicate, how we want to relate to others and how we want to express ourselves.

Maybe you need to become a better listener. Good listeners seldom interrupt. Wait a few seconds when someone has finished talking before you respond. This person may have more to say. This will also help you understand them better. This is not always easy. Sometimes you need to think what has been said, rather than answering at once. Stall a bit by saying "I understand" or "I don't understand, can you explain some more?". And if you are not sure ask for more details. Assumptions are the make of poor communication. Don't rely on mind reading; express your own needs and feelings directly and clearly; ask questions if you don't understand something.

To improve your communication style, an observation period always helps. You could focus on areas that you struggle with, the roles that keep you stuck, and you can understand how you can develop different, more freeing ways that lead to better communication, deeper relationships and self-development.

Feelings of guilt

A lot of people I interviewed told me about feeling guilty because the illness has an impact on their families and they do everything they can to minimise that burden, and all I can think is how toxic the feelings of guilt can be. People do not go on holidays with people they love because they feel guilty that they will alter the holiday plans. They do not drink water so that the carer does not have to help them too many times to the loo. They also talk about feeling guilty over how their condition impacts on others and changes their relationships and this can make it harder for them to ask for support.

Feeling remorse for something wrong that you did, e.g. stealing someone else's idea or hitting someone with the car and abandoning them is unavoidable. The discomfort of the remorse will prevent you from behaving in a similar way in the future. Feelings have a developmental function but guilt about something we have no control of, i.e. our condition and physical limitations, does not serve any purpose.

Listen carefully to your internal principles. Our internal principles help us to control negative aspects of our character and to relate with those around us in a healthy way. Guilt is often related with the unreasonable demands we have of ourselves, the strict morality and low self-esteem.

On the other hand, your partner may also struggle with guilt. Guilt that they can't do enough for you, or they're not doing it well, or guilt when they can go out and enjoy themselves when you can't or simply for being fit and active.

If you put guilt in a Petri dish, it needs three things to grow exponentially: secrecy, silence and judgement. It's important to talk about any feelings of guilt you have and if the condition changes overtime, it is important to keep this conversation open and discuss things as the condition changes. It takes courage to talk frankly about the situation you are both in and what support you need. But it will ease guilty feelings and make both of you more confident.

'I' statements versus 'you' statements

Arguments are built on 'you' messages. This opening phrase structures the assertion that follows so it will be taken personally. 'You' messages come in several forms. They can be critical labels. "You are inconsiderate" is a description of the person's essence and not their surface behaviour. They can be accusations. "You don't care", "you don't realize how I feel", or "you don't pay attention". These are the mind-reading 'you' messages through which we tell the other what he or she is thinking, feeling and believing in the situation. Or they can infer blame. "You made me". These messages are simply dishonest ways of expressing our feelings.

Once we start down the 'you' message path, we leave the other no choice but to react emotionally to our accusations and confrontational style. This path leads nowhere. The problem that started doesn't get solved. Emotionally, however, it makes tremendous sense to us. The upheaval somehow releases us from any responsibility.

When we start using 'you' messages, others generally resist us. They pay us back and use 'you' messages to defend themselves. Things can get very competitive, leading to frustration, and raising anger.

'I' messages, on the other hand, help us stay connected with the other, even in disagreement. 'I' messages are inherently appreciative. They recognise the other positively even when the situation isn't working well.

If you want the other person to change, clearly state what you need them to do. If they argue, repeat your need with the same words and tone, like a broken record. 'I' statements are direct, assertive expressions of your views and feelings. For example, instead of saying "you never listen to me", say "I appreciate when you put your phone away when I talk to you". Instead of saying "You're wrong", how about "I disagree"? Isn't that what you really want to describe – your state of disagreement? You really have no business talking about their 'wrongness'. And what about instead of saying: "You aren't making any sense", say "I don't understand". That's all you can honestly say. The other may think he or she is making pretty good sense from his or her perspective. Also, watch out for hidden 'you' messages with 'I feel . . .' stuck in front of them. For example, "I feel angry when you walk fast", instead you can say "I have a hard time walking fast".

Naturally, like any new skill, using 'I' messages takes time and practice. Start by really listening to yourself and to others. Supermarkets are a good place to hear lots of 'you' messages as parents talk to their children. In your head turn some of the 'you' messages you hear into 'I' messages. You'll be surprised at how fast 'I' messages become a habit.

'I' statements are not a cure-all. Sometimes the listener has to have the time to hear them. This is especially true if the person often hears blaming messages. If using 'I' messages does not work at first, just persevere and continue to use them. Things will change as you gain skills and you begin to break down old patterns of communication.

Some people can use 'I' messages as means of manipulation. They may often express that they are sad, angry, or frustrated in order to gain sympathy from others. If used in this way, problems can escalate. Effective 'I' messages must report honest feelings.

Note finally that 'I' messages are an excellent way to express positive feelings and deliver compliments. For example, "I really appreciate the extra time you gave me today, doctor".

Deepen your relationships

We are born into a web of relationships and spend most of our lives creating, sustaining, or ending them. Central to our emotional and social lives are friendship and long-term romantic relationships. Maintaining a positive connection with another unique person through the ups and downs of life requires real work and the ability to communicate effectively.

It is not uncommon for a long-term condition to have an impact on your relationships with others. I'm not talking here about a negative impact necessarily, but since the long-term condition has changed things for you, it's only natural for your relationships to also shift. Maybe you become more short-tempered with the people you feel closest to, perhaps you think you can no longer relate to people from your golf club, perhaps you feel closer to your children as they have reached out trying to better understand what is happening to you.

Take advantage of these shifts and further develop, nurture and deepen the relationships with others. Asking for help in a specific yet respectful way is one way to connect with others around you to make them feel valued, useful, counted on. Even though most of us will need help on some occasions, few of us like to ask for it. We may not want to be a burden on others. We may hesitate or make a very vague request: "I'm sorry to have to ask this . . ." or "I know this is asking a lot . . ." or "I hate to ask this, but . . .". Hedging like this tends to put the other person on the defensive, and they might think: "Gosh, what's he going to ask that's such a big deal?" To avoid this response, be specific. The person being asked to help may be unable to help appropriately if the request is not clear.

On the other hand, we often hear "how can I help?" Our answer is often "I don't know" or "thank you, but I don't need any help". Be prepared to accept help by having a specific answer. For example, "It would be great, if you could walk my dog on Thursday afternoons when I have physio and I come home late" or "Could you help me change the beddings please, I can't bend and reach over the wall end". Tell people what help you want, and thank them for it. Think about how each person can help you. Give people a task that they can easily accomplish. People like being helpful and feel rejected when they cannot assist someone they care for.

People with health problems sometimes have to deal with offers of support that are neither needed nor desired. In most cases, these offers come from people who genuinely want to help. A well-worded 'I' message allows you to decline the help without embarrassing the other person. "Oh, that's kind of you, but today I think I can manage it myself. I hope I can take you up on your offer another time".

Ask people about their day and take an active interest. But don't fake interest in conversations, this always shows. Find an aspect of what they are telling you that interests you and ask about that. And if you can't find anything of what they say interesting you can always ask how they feel about it, that's always interesting and make others feel heard. Ask about how they felt then and how they feel now.

See the other's perspective and expand your awareness. Sometimes we are so caught up with our thoughts that we forget that other people also have feelings and maybe they too are caught up in their narrative. Their actions are not a threat to us; they act the way they do because they had to deal with unpleasant things in their day – things are not as personal as we make them be.

Other ways to improve your relationships

Here are some ideas of small and easy ways that can have a significant positive impact on your relationships.

- Give presents. Presents are a sign of care and offering and something that gives us joy through giving joy to others.
- Try to remember people's birthdays and important days and send text messages to show that you have them in your thoughts.
- Write letters when you want to express something to someone important to you, and you want to make sure that you can convey your message clearly and thoroughly.
- Don't underestimate/minimise other's efforts to help you or show you support.
- Don't complain but state the facts.
- Show your appreciation with small acts of kindness.
- Be in touch with your feelings and thoughts but do not let them consume you.

- Practice active listening. Don't give your opinion or advice until the other asks. Don't interrupt to debate the other. Don't tell the other what he or she should be thinking or feeling. Don't use the other's story as a take-off for your story.
- Practice non-judging. Before you react, take a time-out and give yourself a chance to become calm. Then ask yourself: Do I have any objective data about what might have contributed to this situation?
- Asserting mindfully. Be confident and considerate. Learn when it is worth arguing for your position and when to let go.
- Use humour but sparingly. On the other hand, don't use sarcasm or demeaning humour, and know when to be serious.

Good communication skills can help make life easier for everyone, especially those with long-term health problems. An appreciative mind-set is a valuable ally. The appreciative mind-set allows us to see the useful, desirable, or positive aspects that already exist in the current situation or in the people present – and to know that these can be revealed, evoked, or realised if we ask the right question. An appreciative view includes valuing and honouring the other while he or she is talking by showing respect, consideration and direct acknowledgement of his or her value. Be sure to ask for the other's input, legitimize his or her feelings, and ask for clarification where appropriate.

A note on living alone

When living alone you do not have people around you that can help you or care for you when you don't feel well. On the other hand, it can feel liberating to do whatever you want, whenever you want. Planning for things might be easier if you don't have other people to consider. You are 'forced' to come up with solutions to your challenges, and since it is you that has to live with the condition, there is no one better to come up with plans.

Let's look in turns the disadvantages and advantages and let's explore some ideas to make these disadvantages lesser and augment the advantages. When you live alone, you don't have people around you to pick up things off the floor, take the bins out or make you dinner when you are feeling unwell. What can you do about that? Can you hire a carer that pops in and checks up on you a couple of time in the day?

Sarah

Sarah was diagnosed in her late teens and always lived on her own. She didn't want to live with anyone else because she wanted to feel free to travel whenever she wanted, wherever she wanted and for however long she wanted. Being diagnosed with lupus did not change that. Now in her late 50s she has found a comfortable pattern of making four or five trips a year within Europe and one or two outside Europe. She had to adjust things and plan more before traveling but she feels very happy and proud that she's managed to carry on with her travelling and she is adamant that having a partner or a family would have slowed her down.

As her condition progressed, she re-designed her house precisely the way she wanted it. She didn't have to consult anyone, and she was able to make quick decisions that were right for her needs and her tastes. This process made her feel very creative and empowered.

Sarah is also very proud that the past two years she has only missed doing her exercises two times. "What helps me to be so disciplined and consistent with my morning work-out is that I have to be self-reliant. I need to stay strong and care for myself. I'm a lazy person when it comes to exercising and if I had someone else around to help, I wouldn't have been so motivated", she says.

If you are alone in the house and you are afraid that you might have an accident and you will be unable to ask for help, have you considered a panic button? This is a device that you can wear around your neck or have by your bed, and if you fall or you need help you press it and this will notify a friend, a family member or a neighbour and they will come over. There might be other devices that might be more appropriate for you; talk to your doctor, nurse or occupational therapist about your fears and they will have some suggestions for you.

Having a long-term condition can be a very isolating experience. There are days you are feeling unwell, you may be upset because you can no longer do the things you used to enjoy. It is only natural to feel that people do not understand you and you're left to deal with it all on your own. How could you make that less true? Most of the times people don't talk to you or avoid asking you questions about your condition because they don't know what to say. They are afraid of saying the wrong thing. Could you initiate meetings with friends and family? Maybe you'll have to do a bit of the initial organising of a place that will be appropriate for you, a restaurant that caters to your dietary needs or that is easy to access with a wheelchair or that you have been to before so that you know exactly where to sit to be close to the bathroom. After that you can let your friends and family know the ideal place for you to meet; this might be your home. You can always take turns to make arrangements for meeting up.

Give people cues or say outright what things you'd like to discuss. Sometimes you might want to talk about your condition; sometimes you might want to talk about everything else. Most of all, let them know that you are still you; maybe your body has limits now, but you are still their friend.

You might find that some of your old friends do not want to accommodate to your needs. They might be self-centred. They may have different priorities. That's fine. That's their life, it's not your life. Do you really want to spend your time with them anyway? As we saw in Chapter 5, a lot of the long-term conditions have a symptom in common: fatigue. You need to spend your energy wisely. This might mean cutting out people who drug you down. This will create more space for the people you want in your circle.

Make it a priority at least once a week to meet up with a friend or a family member, even if you don't really feel like it. A lot of the times, you will end up enjoying yourself. Cultivating relationships are important for our psychological well-being and quality of life and having people close by will make it easier to reach out for help when you need to. Going on holidays together with friends or family can also be an excellent opportunity for you to bond and get closer. Let alone . . . you know . . . having fun! Setting dates for meeting your friends or having planned holidays are also great for building in some anticipation and excitement into your days. You have things to look forward to, things you will enjoy, and they will also create beautiful memories for you for the years to come. A central notion of this book is finding ways to make your condition have less of an influence over the things you want to do. Being with other people could achieve just that.

Have you thought of attending local groups of people with your condition? Charities and volunteer groups usually organise regular meet-ups. To find out more you could check the relevant charity's website or even the meet-up.com page to see if you can find any relevant group close to you. This suggestion might not be for everyone. Especially if you are early on in the diagnosis you might not want to be associated with such groups or you might not want to be around people who have had the condition for a long time. That's very understandable. You might just want to go once to see what it's all about. A lot of people have found such groups very helpful. They can make you feel understood and less alone and you might find it easier to discuss matters related to the condition that you could not talk about with your family and close friends; you can also learn some tips about managing the condition. Of course, if you attend those groups you will hear things that might not be applicable to you or that are not helpful for your situation, but you never know where the next great piece of advice will be coming from, so better to be prepared.

Georgina

> Georgina was very reluctant to attend any such groups. She was diagnosed with the condition in her 40s and she did not want to go to a group with people who will probably be much older than her. Also, her symptoms were mild and under control, so she didn't feel the need to attend those groups or identify with them. However, a few years later, when her local Parkinson's group invited a neurologist, she decided to attend. During the coffee break she talked to other people with Parkinson's, mostly people who had just been diagnosed and were very distressed about the prognosis, hence they attended the talk. She talked to them about her experience and this calmed them considerably. She felt it was important to help others and by being part of this group she could help others and learn something for herself. She formally joined the group and since then, she has reduced her working hours and undertaken the secretary role organising monthly events specifically for those newly diagnosed with Parkinson's.

Communicating with health professionals

Whether you want your doctor to make all the calls regarding your treatment plan or you want to know all the details and have a say about the best treatment for you, you will get more from your interactions with medical professionals if you improve the way you communicate with them. In particular, it is vital that your doctors, nurses and other health care professionals understand you and that equally you understand them. When you don't understand advice or recommendations from your doctor or health team, the resulting lack of clarity can be life threatening. So, for a self-manager, effective communication skills are essential.

The General Medical Council published a short booklet in 2013 called, "What to expect from your doctor: a guide for patients". It recognises that it can be difficult to take in all the information the doctor is sharing with you and recommends that you ask for clarification. It cites examples of questions surrounding your medication, how you should take it and how to prepare for any tests you may need to undergo.

To help the communication with the doctors, first of all you must be clear about what you want from them and the health care system. Undoubtedly, you have felt frustrated, angry, or depressed from time to time about your condition. Doctors have probably felt similar emotions about their inability to make you well. In this sense, you are truly partners.

If you live in the UK, you probably have to wait a long time to get an appointment with a specialist and once you're in their office, time runs out before you know it. To make the most of your precious little time with the health care professional you should prepare prior to your appointment. Make yourself an agenda. What are the issues that bother you the most? Prioritise the most important things you want to discuss. Give relevant details and be open about them. If something is unclear or you don't understand, ask. Don't hold back. It might also be useful to repeat what you have just been told to make sure you understood it right, but this will also help you to retain the information. If you feel particularly nervous about an appointment, ask someone close to you to join you. Not only will you have a second pair of ears to listen to what the doctors say but also someone to talk to about the appointment afterwards. Make it an event. Grab a cup of coffee and spend some time with your spouse or friend who accompanied you in the appointment.

Before you leave the doctor's office make sure you are clear about the next steps. Where do you need to go, what needs to be done, what medication you need, how to obtain it and how to take it. Ask your doctor to write the next steps down for you or give you a leaflet that explains the next steps to take with you.

Discuss problems and brainstorm solutions with health care professionals. Then practice and come back to the health care professional to discuss the success or lack of success of the solution. If you haven't solved the problem in the first go there is no reason to feel disheartened, you have collected good information on potential barriers and on what might or might not work for you and your lifestyle. Armoured with this new information you can now go back to the health care professional and discuss the potential barriers, what worked and what did not and how to move forward with your plan.

Asking your doctor questions

- Ask directly.
- Paraphrase what you have heard to check that you have understood correctly.
- Avoid asking why and instead ask who, which, when or where.
- Avoid asking closed questions for which the answer will be a simple yes or no; if you do so follow on with a who, which, when or where question.
- Don't pose double-barrel or multiple questions at once, because your doctor/nurse/etc is likely to remember and answer the first or the last of them; instead ask one thing at a time.
- Specific versus general questions. The more specific the question, the clearer the answer you'll get. On the other hand, general questions could lead to longer and more meaningful conversations because they invite conversation, opinions and unexpected turns of discourse.

Communicating with your partner

Your partner can be a real help when you are managing a long-term condition. Your partner might feel empowered when supporting you in staying as active, fulfilled and in control of your life as possible. And there are things you can do to support your partner too and help them cope. Your relationship can become deeper than before.

Your partner's reaction to the diagnosis might be different to yours. Some people go into denial, push away those close to them or seem to give up. Maybe this is their way of processing what is happening and getting control over things. Everyone moves on to acceptance at their own pace. Knowing that these reactions are their way of coming to terms with the diagnosis can help you take things less personally. Give them some time to process the new information in their own time. Offer to help them get some good quality information about the condition, make sure they know you are there and open to discuss things when they feel ready and try not to take their reactions personally. In some cases, you might need to see a counsellor or psychologist if things are getting really difficult or if you or your partner find it difficult to come to terms with the condition.

You both face having to change your hopes for the future, and that can be unsettling. The hardest thing can be losing who you both felt you were before the diagnosis. You grieve for the loss of how things used to be and for what you think you'll never have. This grief can be seen as a journey through different reactions; shock or denial, guilt, anger, bargaining, depression, acceptance and hope.

People go back and forth between different stages. There's no one way or right way. Each person goes through these stages in their own way and it may take time. You can rush things or force things to happen. Open up some space to these emotions, let them be with you for as long or as little as they are there. You can also share with each other what things you do that help you cope.

Fear is another common emotion not only for you but also for your family. Some people may want to read lots about the condition, whereas others will want to know as little as possible. It is important to get information about the condition that you can trust and get it when you need it most. It'll help both you and your family to understand better what the future may hold. A long-term condition can put relationships to the test. If you're feeling fearful and uncertain you might feel less like talking and this also might be true for your partner. But now is the time when good communication will help you both find a way through.

Sometimes, when dealing with a long-term condition, it can be tough to keep communication open. Everyone is different. There's no 'route map' to tell us what we should go through or how to manage it. But how do you talk to someone truthfully without upsetting them or making them angry?

If you need your partner to change, you need to assertively ask for it and ask in a voice that communicates courage, calm and clarity. The three main ingredients of assertive communication are: staying present, speaking up descriptively, and asking for change.

When disagreements arise, people are not listening they are reacting, so you have to say it again. Then, if your partner comes at you with criticism, acknowledge his or her truth. If your partner behaves aggressively, he or she expects direct resistance. Try to sidestep their anger by agreeing with some part of what he or she says.

As you progress towards some sort of resolution of a situation, you will find additional connective statements helpful. Try a situational acknowledgement: "I know this has been tough on both of us". Or how about a blameless apology? "I'm so sorry this has happened". Finally, you can use a situational requirement description: "What else can we do? Your mother is coming on Friday". The goal is to reach an agreement to change – that works for you and your partner – without beating up yourself or your partner.

When your partner seems to have put it all on the table, you can break in gently and say, "OK, do you mind if I tell my side of the story?" Seeking permission shows respect and reinforces equality, which is the basis for effective dialogue. As you're talking, ask for occasional feedback on your words; give and get clarification until you're satisfied he or she understands your side of the story.

Choose the time and the place carefully when you want to clear out a misunderstanding. Avoid important conversations if you're angry, tired or in a bad mood. When the time feels right, turn off the TV, your phone and other distractions. Look the other person in the eye and listen to them the way you'd like to be listened to. Let them finish speaking before answering. Say how you feel without either of you feeling guilty or responsible.

In a couple each partner often takes on certain roles. One might be the talker, the practical one, the planner, the provider, the one who looks after the other or the one who gets looked after. A long-term condition can change these roles suddenly or over time. You may need to cut back your work hours, or no longer do the more physical chores at home. These changes can make you both feel disappointed, frustrated and like you've lost something.

Get support through family or friends, if that's possible. You might turn down help to keep up the appearance that everything's OK. Maybe you think friends and family won't understand the condition, or you don't want to be a burden. If you feel you're doing any of these, talk it through with them. Don't be scared to approach people again for help. We all need a support network. This will help you and your partner. De-stress with things you enjoy: hobbies, exercise, being with family, walking the dog, cooking, yoga, music and so on. Are you or your partner feeling down? Possibly depressed? Worried about how you're coping? Start by talking to someone. Your GP can help get the help you need. Counselling can help. A lot of charities have a helpline for emotional support that you can contact.

One thing worth trying is a regular meeting or 'family time' when you're all encouraged to ask questions; you can include your children if they are old enough. That way everyone understands better what's going on. It might feel strange at first and you might worry people's feelings will get hurt. But with more of these 'family time' meetings confidence often grows until you can talk about very sensitive topics as well as resolve situations before they even become an issue.

The lack of structure in daily life, usually imposed by the conditions' unpredictable symptoms or the treatment schedules, can make things more difficult for everyone in the family. Symptoms such as fatigue mean that what a person could do yesterday they might struggle with today. Planning can be tricky when you're not sure what the next day, week or month might bring. Changes of plan like this often happen with little or no warning. You can lessen their impact if you talk about what you'd do if plans change. Build in flexibility. Encourage everyone to be creative about how to do what you planned but in a different way.

It also helps if you have back-up plans. Having back-up plans can prevent disappointment, anger or frustration. As a matter of fact, don't stop making plans. Having positive things happening in the future for you both to look forward to not only improves mood and relationships but builds memories that will last and help you through rough patches.

So how do we know if we are in a satisfying long-term relationship? Here are the three key characteristics of such relationships:

- Investment. We – and the other – give our time, energy and mental focus to building and sustaining the relationship.
- Commitment. As a result of our continued investment in the recent past, we believe in the future of the relationship.
- Trust. Trust is built by each of us being dependable and keeping our promises.

When the partner is also a carer

There are 6.5 million carers in the UK, with 80% of partners of people with a disabling condition providing over 50 hours of care per week.[7] Informal caregivers, as spouses and partners, also need to adjust their lives and provide help to their partners such as personal care, organising leisure activities and removing physical and emotional barriers so the person with the illness can carry on their usual activities. All these extra activities may lead to more stress for the caregivers. At the same time caregivers also report benefits from their experiences, such as increased confidence, pride, gratification, personal achievement and feeling closer to their spouse.

There are a lot of people who wouldn't call themselves a 'carer' or they don't really like the word. Instead they say "I'm a partner, daughter, son, mother, father or friend". What they do for the person they look after grows out of that relationship. Most people don't plan on becoming a carer. It usually happens slowly, although sometimes it happens overnight. They might take on a few responsibilities that put them under no extra pressure. But after a relapse or medical emergency they might give a lot more support. Then it's good to know what help is available.

Identifying as a carer can give them a way into lots of support, making it possible for them to carry on being a carer (if that's what they want to do). The law says carers have a right to a Carers' Assessment. This is when your local council looks at what help you need. In Northern Ireland your local Health and Social Care Trust does this. This could mean extra practical support or money. You can find out about Carers' Assessments at www.carersuk.org. Also, carers need to let their GP know.

Communicating with your children

There are no set rules about when and how to talk to your children about the condition. Factors like the nature of your condition, the impact on usual family life, the age of your children, other family circumstances and your relationship with your children will all influence how and when you will talk to them.

But it is difficult to hide things from children. They notice subtle changes in mood and hushed conversations as clues that something is not right. If they feel left out, they may make up their own story, which may well be far worse than the truth. They may sense that the cause for concern is secret and so don't share their distress. For some children, this can be expressed in their behaviour, schoolwork or friendships. There is also the possibility that if you don't tell them, they might find out some other way.

It'll be for the best if they're allowed to understand the condition better and ask questions. When a parent has a long-term condition, children benefit from knowing more about it and how it affects their mum or dad. In the long run things work out better when kids are part of important decisions and parents talk with their children – whatever their age – about future plans.

The good news is that when you include your children in discussions, when they are encouraged to talk about their own feelings and are made to feel that their opinions matter, they will grow up to be as happy and well-adjusted as other children. They will also grow up with a better understanding of health and how to cope with negative emotions. Children need to be able to trust you and being honest with them helps them to do that. Keeping things hidden can be a great strain.

Choosing to talk to your children about the condition can be a complex decision. As a parent, you know your circumstances and your own children best. You are the best judge of how to discuss your health with your family, and when it is the best time to do it, knowing that there is no ideal time.

Find an easy way to explain to your children the condition, giving them descriptions that they can understand. There are a lot of children's books that you can use to explain things, or you can ask professionals to help you with the task. You don't want to create any mystery or stigma around the condition or the symptoms, so be matter-of-fact. Keep conversations open and honest to discuss with your child what he or she feels comfortable with and make sure they get the support they need.

Children can be very supportive and may surprise you by doing or saying something which shows how they understand. Not all children will be understanding; some may appear unconcerned about your condition and, like some adults, try to ignore it. Other children may express hostility or become withdrawn.

It is important to take the lead in talking about the condition. Some children will not ask questions, even if they are worried, for fear of upsetting you or because they feel the topic is 'off limits'. Several factors affect your readiness to have a first talk and many parents prefer not to have a 'formal' talk at all.

The first talk you have with your children about your condition is important. It opens up the topic for discussion and sets the tone for further conversations about the condition. Children soon realise if you would rather not talk to them and will think they can't talk to you. If you are falsely positive, they might think they can't admit to their own negative feelings. It is better to admit that you don't have all the answers; if you tell them things that are not true, they may find out and feel unable to believe your reassurances in the future.

If you have more than one child it may be best to begin by telling them all together so that they start with the same information, at the same time. You can talk to them individually at a later date, as and when they need to.

That first conversation needn't cover everything about your condition. Keep it simple. The most important message is to reassure them that, whilst things might change, you love and care for them now and always. It is often useful to ask them what they know about your condition so you can correct any misunderstandings.

Children of different ages will have different concerns; whereas toddlers may be worried that you will have to go to the hospital and experience separation anxiety, school-age children may need re-assurance that your condition was not caused by and had nothing to do with them. Adolescents may also worry about whether the condition is hereditary and whether they may get it.

Some children seem to accept a short chat and are quick to return to the next activity. If that is the case don't push them to talk as they may need to think things through over a longer period of time. The important message is that all their feelings and questions are OK and that the health condition can be talked about as much or as little as they need.

As they grow up their own understanding of the health condition will change, and they may want more details so it's important to keep the lines of communication open. You know when your children are most likely to talk and the best conversations may happen at meal times, in the car or at bath time.

It is not unusual for children to feel more comfortable turning to the parent who isn't diagnosed with the condition for support, to a grandparent or a close friend. They may also talk to brothers or sisters when they don't want to talk to parents.

Sometimes children may ask questions that shock or upset you. Whilst it is important to be open and honest with your children it is essential that they don't stop asking questions for fear of upsetting you. If one of their questions or comments takes you by surprise it might be helpful to say something like "that's a good question – I need a bit of time to think about that one, can we talk about it later?" This will give you time to deal with your immediate emotional response and think about how to respond as well as let your children know that they can ask about uncomfortable topics. It's important that your children know they can talk freely about your condition and all their associated feelings.

The evidence shows that children are resilient and can cope with an enormous amount when adults are open and honest and children are made to feel that their feelings and opinions are important. Everybody experiences negative feelings in life. All children need to learn to cope with upsetting situations. Giving your children the skills to understand and express their negative emotions about your condition will give them a good resource for life.

Some children will seem completely unaffected by a parent's diagnosis; others may become more withdrawn or show changes in their behaviour. All these reactions are normal, and children need to be reassured that whatever they are feeling is reasonable and the same as other children would feel.

You and your family can help them most by expressing your own feelings. A partner might say "it makes me sad that Mum can't come and see your play today, I wish she was feeling better". A parent with a long-term condition might say "I've been feeling so tired today, I just didn't have the energy to hang the washing out. I was so angry with myself!" Conversations like this will let them see that other people in the family sometimes feel negative things and it is fine for them to say when they feel angry or upset about the long-term condition.

A long-term condition is different for each person and each family. Children will not necessarily exhibit more emotional and behavioural issues when compared to children of families without a long-term condition. When kids are part of a larger family, there is less need for them to carry out important caring jobs. But in smaller families some will do most of the care and support for the parent with a long-term condition.

This caring role could affect relationships with friends and schoolwork. It might be a good idea to contact social services in the UK or social work in Scotland. These services will do a 'Carers assessment'. The carers assessment will help you identify what extra support the young person might need.

Not every child or young person with a parent with a long-term condition ends up being a 'young carer'. However, children might take on household jobs like washing, cleaning and shopping. However, carrying out more personal care tasks for their mum or dad puts pressure on them. Where possible it's better if someone else does these. Studies have shown that some caring tasks can have a beneficial effect for children, like providing emotional support for their parent or help out with age-appropriate practical household chores, e.g. paying bills and doing grocery shopping, whereas caring tasks like providing personal care, bathing and feeding the parent might be best to be left for someone else to do.

Young people may have questions that they don't feel comfortable asking their parents. Some families say it helps if schools or colleges are told that the young person is caring for someone with a long-term condition. Others are relieved when their child joins a local young carers' group as this means that their child can get support and information.

Helping people close to you adjust

Everyone is happier when they feel their needs are being met. Therefore, your partner or maybe your children are helping you out with practical aspects, helping you in and out of bed or taking up more of the house chores when you have a flare up, but what is it that you can offer them? Your illness might be all consuming, the symptoms might be overwhelming but is there time in your day that you can direct your focus to the ones close to you. This time might not be too long or too frequent, but you can make it count. Pretend that you are a brain with two eyes, looking outwards. Connecting with the human being close to you, taking in the world, being interested in the world. Be curious about them, their day, their relationships, their problems. Listen carefully and compassionately. Offer some advice if you genuinely have some thoughts or suggestions for their issues. Try to identify activities that you can still enjoy together; this might be as simple as reading a book to each other or more organised like attending a course together.

If your condition is likely to deteriorate, can you make arrangements to help your partner or children in the future? For example, can you meet with a finance advisor to get some help on how you can save money, how to invest money etc so that your partner will not have this additional financial stress to worry about? Maybe you can identify external carers, trial them and have them on stand-by so that you can reach out to them for help if you need to or if your partner wants to have a respite. Or maybe you need to plan the purchase of any equipment you might need in the future, such as a stair lift, kitchen modifications or changing your bathroom into a wet room.

People with a long-term condition, especially progressive conditions, need much information about the condition and how to manage it early on during the diagnosis; family members want more support and information later on in the trajectory. Find out what they need to know, explain things to them, make it explicit that it is OK to ask you anything about the condition. You get the idea – whatever it is that you think you might need in the future that will help your partner directly or that will help you retain some independence and indirectly help your partner.

Your social network

Having a social network helps us to feel that we are cared for; we belong to a network and mutually can expect others to assist us. Such relationships can buffer the effects of stress and promote well-being. A social network includes relationships with family, friends and health care professionals, face-to-face or via telephone or internet.

In our networks, we need more than a couple of people, and that can be as little or as many as you feel comfortable with. You need people who can help with different types of things. People who can provide you with different kinds of help. You need people who can help with tangible support, or financial or physical assistance. You need people who can provide you with advice and guidance on specific issues, and you need people who can help you emotionally, people that you can seek comfort from or exchange coping stories, perhaps someone who is in a similar situation.

Support from your community or other people with the same condition can help you maintain the knowledge, skills and confidence to self-manage. You can access this support when you need to and can help with things that healthcare professionals can't, like loneliness and confidence.[5] People who have a high degree of support from family and friends are healthier and live longer than people who do not,[8] and they are more likely to accept their condition.[9]

Look at your personal values from Chapter 2, to remind yourself what is important to you and what you want to achieve through boosting the bonds with your family and friend. Make a list of your current network:

Person	Relationship	Notes on current status

Do you feel you need more people in your life or are you satisfied with your current network?

If you are not satisfied:

- What steps can you take towards adding more people in your list (see also guidelines on action planning in Chapter 3 to help you design your self-management plan)?
- What small actionable steps you can take starting now to add more people in your network?

If you are satisfied with the current number of people:

- Which relationships do you want to prioritise for the time being to nurture and cultivate further?
- What small actionable steps you can take starting now to improve these relationships?

Bibliography

1 Duck S. *Relating to Others*. Open University Press; 1999.
2 Cohen S, Doyle WJ, Skoner DP, Frank E, Rabin BS, Gwaltney JM. Types of Stressors That Increase Susceptibility to the Common Cold in Healthy Adults. *Health Psychology*. 1998;17(3):214–223. doi:10.1037/0278-6133.17.3.214
3 Kiecolt-Glaser JK, Loving TJ, Stowell JR, et al. Hostile Marital Interactions, Proinflammatory Cytokine Production, and Wound Healing. *Archives of General Psychiatry*. 2005;62(12):1377–1384. doi:10.1001/archpsyc.62.12.1377
4 Newsom JT, Rook KS, Nishishiba M, Sorkin DH, Mahan TL. Understanding the Relative Importance of Positive and Negative Social Exchanges: Examining Specific Domains and Appraisals. *Journals Gerontol: Series B Psychological Sciences and Social Sciences*. 2005;60(6). doi:10.1093/geronb/60.6.P304
5 *A Practical Guide to Self-Management Support*. Health Foundation. https://reader.health.org.uk/practical-guide-to-self-management-support/what-is-self-management-support-and-why-is-it-important. Accessed December 15, 2019.
6 Goleman D. *Emotional Intelligence: 10th Anniversary Edition*. Bantam; 2012.
7 Ostwald SK. Who Is Caring for the Caregiver? *Family & Community Health*. 2009;32(Supplement):S5–S14. doi:10.1097/01.FCH.0000342835.13230.a0
8 Berkman LF, Glass T, Brissette I, Seeman TE. From Social Integration to Health: Durkheim in the New Millennium. *Social Science and Medicine*. 2000;51(6):843–857. doi:10.1016/S0277-9536(00)00065-4
9 Pakenham KI, Fleming M. Relations between Acceptance of Multiple Sclerosis and Positive and Negative Adjustments. *Psychology & Health*. 2011;26(10):1292–1309. doi:10.1080/08870446.2010.517838

Chapter 8

Designing the life you want

The key message of this book is that managing a long-term condition is not an all-consuming activity. And a long-term condition does not necessarily have to take up every waking moment of your life. Making some time to sharpen your self-management tools – many of which are described in this book – will save you time and energy that you could then spend on things that are truly important to you. Living well means spending time on things that matter.

Kathryn

Kathryn discovered she had Multiple Sclerosis in her mid 30's she has a young daughter, 3-years-old, and is pregnant with her second daughter. She is a primary school teacher and lives with her husband and daughter. During her pregnancy, her MS symptoms have subsided a lot. She's feeling great. However, she is afraid that once she has the baby, a bad relapse will be around the corner, and she won't be able to care for her newborn. This is the reason why she wants to complete as many tasks as possible now while spending as much time as possible with her daughter, which not only leaves her exhausted but her anxiety to get everything done keeps her awake at night. Also, she's struggling with worry about what the future holds for her and her family. Multiple Sclerosis is progressive and is unpredictable. She never knows when she will get the next relapse, how severe it will be, how long it will last, and whether she will recover completely from it or not. Adding to the mix, two young children and a demanding job make the juggling of all components extra challenging.

To better self-manage her condition, Kathryn wants to manage better her fatigue, her difficulties with sleeping and work on increasing her uncertainty tolerance. To set herself up for success, she focused on one of these areas – avoiding doing too much and all at once. The first area she wanted to focus on was her sleep, as she thought this was the symptom that had the worst impact on her quality of life. Her ultimate goal was feeling rested when waking up. She wanted to take some steps towards that bigger, long-term goal.

Before putting together the plan on how to address her sleep difficulties, she wanted to find out her big WHY. To connect with her values that drove her decision to give up energy and time to manage her sleep difficulties better. To find the WHY that fuels her efforts and that will keep her motivated when things get tough. Her big WHY was that she wanted to have enough energy to accomplish everything she wanted to and feel proud of herself. Think about her big WHY made her excited and inspired her. She felt like she was willing to jump through hoops and stop at nothing to achieve that goal.

She decided to establish a relaxing bedtime routine that included a shower, a short breathing practice and listening to an audiobook in bed. Also, she moved her focus away from how much or little she slept each night and started recording how much energy she had during the day. Each evening, she planned the day, which included activities that made her happy and accomplished and also tried to include some form of physical activity. She also booked an appointment with her Multiple Sclerosis nurse to get any other recommendations and discuss whether her medications might have anything to do with her difficulties sleeping.

After a few months, when she saw some progress on feeling more rested, Kathryn also decided to take advantage of the fact that she felt more energetic during the morning. She saw a poster at a local flower shop on classes on flower arrangement. The course ran for six weeks, on Saturdays at 8 a.m. Usually, her Saturday mornings were spent in bed trying and failing to catch up on sleep and then feeling sluggish and low throughout the day. Now she had a purpose every Saturday morning to get out of bed. She felt proud of herself. She got ready, out of the door, completed a lesson and had some breakfast at nearby café and all that before most people had got out of bed. This course was something that not only made her feel accomplished but gave her the chance to exercise her creativity.

Her success in managing her difficulties with sleep boosted her confidence and strengthened her belief that she can keep on top of her symptoms. Her partner had also noticed differences in her energy levels. And positive outlook and full days, made her feel so proud of her achievement.

However, worrying about the future hasn't changed. Very frequently, she felt anxious. Still, she tried not to let her anxiety overwhelm her and take over. She was concerned, but she was also able to play with her daughter. She was able to speak with her mom on the phone while also feeling anxiety. And the more she learned to do things alongside her concern, the less she felt threatened by it.

Be clear about your symptoms and their psychological impact

Identify things that have changed and things you might like to change. Unravelling all the difficulties involved can be extremely valuable. Looking at their impact and how they compare with other challenges can give us a clearer picture of how to deal with them. Create a list of things you want to change or cope with, then prioritise the items. Which challenge do you want to address first, and which problem can stay unresolved? Identifying and carefully prioritising your needs is the vital first step.

Identify your values to guide your self-management plans

But why do you want to make changes? If you're going to make changes, what motivates you to make those changes? Identifying your values will help you refine your aims in life. Having clear goals can direct your choices on which activities to include in your life to make it happier and more meaningful. It is not always necessary to have specific goals; some events are worth doing just for the sheer pleasure of doing them. We nourish our soul when we lose ourselves to pastimes without always aiming to accomplish anything in particular. If you can't think of 'just for fun' activities, think of things you used to enjoy when you were a child. The key is that all these activities align with your values.

Manage your stress to limit its impact

Sometimes, when we have some difficulty in certain areas of our lives, an overwhelming feeling can infuse all other areas. We generalise, we feel like everything is wrong, and nothing can be done. It is OK; we all do this.

Steps to managing your symptoms

Identify the most troubling symptoms. Talk to your medical team about them and get some advice on how they can be resolved. It is not uncommon for symptoms to be left untreated just because it is uncomfortable talking about them with a health professional.

Then make a specific plan of how you would like to tackle the symptom. What, when, where, how often. Make sure you have the resources you need to realise your plan.

Put your plan into action for a few days or weeks, depending on the frequency of the activity, then review your plan. Did you get the results you were hoping for? And if it wasn't as successful, you have probably identified what you need to tweak to make it more successful or at least you have collected some information that you can take back to the health professional you initially talked to and ask for further advice and guidance. The more specific details the health professionals have, the easier it is for them to come up with ideas and solutions to help you out.

Once you have modified your plan and you are more aware of potential barriers, it's time to work on your Plan B. Using if-then structure, make plans of how you will overcome your obstacles. If I feel stressed, **then** I will call my brother before heading to the kitchen.

Sharpen up your psychological skills

Having some psychological tricks up your sleeves can help you manage your symptoms but also using them can make you feel better. I am calling these psychological **skills** because as with other skills, you can acquire them, and by practising, you can become better.

The most important of these skills is what psychologists call self-efficacy: the belief that you have what it takes to achieve your goals. Research studies have found that self-efficacy is the most potent factor associated with better psychological adjustment to a long-term condition.

There are four different ways you can increase this confidence in your abilities to perform what you set out to do successfully.

First, by thinking of your successes, current and past. There might be successes related to managing your condition; achievements in other areas in your life can also have a spillover effect on your confidence in your ability to achieve your health managing related goals.

Second, you can increase your belief in yourself by identifying people in similar circumstances with you (online or in real life) that have achieved what you want to make. You not only get motivated by other successes, but you can also see their journey to success. Surround yourself with people who have achieved what you want to make, observe them and get inspired.

Having other people encourage you along the way can also help increase your confidence. Find a 'buddy' to be your cheerleader, someone you can talk to about the ups and downs of your journey that you know will encourage you and support you. It can be a close family member or someone who is also trying to manage their condition better, so you can help each other. You can even encourage yourself along the way by leaving motivational post-it notes throughout your house as a visual reminder that you can do it or by writing down some positive self-affirmations.

And last but not least, the better we feel in general, the more confident we also think. Managing your negative thoughts and emotions will make it easier for you to feel more confident in your abilities.

Thoughts matter. How you talk about yourself – and to yourself – can affect how your brain functions. Even the words you think without ever saying them affect your brain and your body, all the time, whether you're aware of these effects or not. We all engage in an almost continuous inner monologue. Every day, thousands of thoughts pass through our stream of consciousness. By altering the flow of that stream of self-talk, it seems we can change our behaviours, our emotions and even our physical health.

After a thought pops in your mind and before you react, take a breath or maybe a few breaths. Taking a breathing space is always the first step in dealing with a thought. With breathing comes an awareness that allows for a more excellent choice about how to respond. We have several options. We can either watch the thoughts come and go with awareness and without feeling that we have to follow them. Or we can view thoughts as mental events instead of facts and decide whether they are true or not. Once we assess the thoughts, we can choose which thoughts to act on and which to let pass by. Just remember, you have a choice. Paying careful attention can give us a different perspective of our problems so that they can, in turn, become less stressful for us.

Awareness of pessimistic or hopeless thought patterns can help us experience fewer downward mood spirals. For every thought, we have choices of what to believe about them or what we can do (if anything) to change things. And if there is nothing you can do about a negative thought, could you let it be? Make space for it and while it is around don't over-identify with it, don't feed it with more negative thoughts. Less engagement with the thoughts will help with having a less emotionally charged experience, and it might also help make letting go of these feelings and thoughts easier.

The feeling of control is an essential element of happiness – a better predictor of happiness than, say, income. Having a sense of autonomy, of being able to choose what happens in your life or how you spent your time, is crucial.

Based on how we have been brought up and our experience, we develop an internal or external explanation of why things turn out the way they do, internal versus external locus of control in psychological terms.

People with an internal locus of control believe their actions and decisions guide their behaviour. People with an external locus of control believe that their conduct is governed by fate, luck or other external factors. People with an internal locus of control have better psychological well-being and are generally more likely to achieve their goals. Because they believe they are in control of their destiny, they are eager to tackle challenges, while those with an external locus of control are apt to say "Why bother? It doesn't matter what I do anyway".

Most people sit somewhere in between the continuum of the two opposite ends. And the good news is that you can change your locus of control and move more towards internal explanations of your behaviour. The key is to use the problem-solving techniques discussed in this book to help you seize control of your life and tackle symptoms or other challenges that come your way.

When faced with a problem you could take a more analytical approach, discussed in Chapter 1, and get as much information as you can about the issue. Then think about your desired outcome. How would you measure success? What exactly do you want to achieve? These first two steps are essential. There are different aspects within each issue; some of them can be solved; some of them can't. For example, in experiencing pain, you might not be able to stop feeling the pain, but you might be able to control your thoughts and amend your behaviours in ways that don't exacerbate the pain, or your goal might be not letting the pain take over your life.

As a third step, you come up with two or more potential solutions to the problem, weigh the pros and cons and decide which one is the best course of action. Pick a solution and put it into practice. Reflect on what is working and what it is not. Modify your efforts and try again. You repeat the cycle of reflection-modification and action as many times as necessary to achieve your goal. It also helps to leave the emotion out of this process as much as possible. Think of the different issues objectively: what is wrong, how do you want to fix it, what are the best ways to do so? If you let emotions slip into the process, they can distort the dimensions of the problems and prevent you from coming up with solutions.

But when you have a long-term condition, you don't only face problems that can be solved but also issues that have no solutions. And recognising which problems can be solved and which can't is not always obvious and frequently it comes with experience. For example, low energy levels might be something that you can address to a certain extent or not at all; similarly deterioration of the condition.

A brain is a problem-solving machine and it needs to predict problems that may or may not happen and find solutions. When solutions are not readily available, this will trigger uncomfortable emotions with the view to urging the brain to come up with solutions to various problems. When we have a long-term condition it puts the mind in overdrive. The brain tries to help out but is not always helping. In other words, worrying about the uncertain future makes you believe that you have more control and certainty in life. In reality, has your worrying made anything more specific or predictable? Does worrying change the outcome of what will happen?

There is a lot to be said about acceptance and the role it plays in adjusting to physical illnesses. Even when taking into consideration illness variables and other demographic and social factors, people who report higher acceptance also feel happier and report less severe symptoms.

Accepting means merely allowing space for whatever is going on, rather than trying to create some other state. Through acceptance, we settle back into awareness of what is present. We let it be – we merely notice and observe whatever is already present.

Accepting difficulties is not resignation. Resignation is passive. Acceptance allows us to become fully aware of problems, and then, if appropriate, to respond skilfully, rather than to react, by automatically running some of our old (and maybe unhelpful) strategies for dealing with difficulties.

By trying to solve an insoluble problem, or by refusing to accept the reality of our situation, we may end up exhausting ourselves and increase our sense of helplessness. In practice, the more we try to control certain things, the more uncontrollable they may become. It will undoubtedly be impossible to control symptoms all of the time.

In summary, the number one skill is **the belief in your abilities**. Another vital skill is **problem-solving**, which will also lead you to increase your **sense of control** over your actions. And for issues that cannot be solved, **acceptance** can help you move past the issue and lead a full life while allowing the issue to be in your life.

Healthy Habits

Having a long-term condition means your body works extra hard to retain a healthy equilibrium. Forming some healthy habits can make the job of the body a little easier, plus you will be reducing the risk of acquiring any additional health issues. Learning ways to help you adhere to your medical regime, exercise more and make healthier food choices will move you towards a healthier body.

Habits are automatic responses to situational cues. The three critical aspects of habits are that they are outside of our awareness, they are beyond our control and are mentally efficient. When it comes to habits, the intention is not of the essence; thinking and planning are not much use, and environmental cues direct our behaviour. To form a habit, you need to link your target behaviour to something that is already a well-established part of your routine – plan to repeat the action until it feels 'automatic'. There is no clear-cut length of time that it will take to form the behaviour. It depends on how frequently the behaviour is performed. If there is something that you need to do monthly, it will take longer to become a habit to something that you perform three times a day. Also, if your new practice is something not too different from what you are currently doing, it will take less time for the new behaviour to become automatic.

Committing to performing the new behaviour on cue for a length of time is not enough. To make sure you're putting in the right effort in forming this new behaviour, you also need to monitor your success or lack of progress, tweak it if necessary and re-evaluate. The monitoring of the practice does not have to be anything fancy, a simple cross on the kitchen calendar to indicate that you have completed the behaviour will give you a good overview of how well you've done. There are also a lot of free apps you can use to help you monitor your habits.

You can use a similar process for when you want to replace a habit. First, you have to identify the cue. What triggers the habit? You can then replace the habit with a more desired one on the same cue. For example, going for a walk when stressed instead of baking and eating cakes. Alternatively, you can change the prompt. For example, stop drinking coffee in the morning to help you quit smoking. The idea is to make it as easy for yourself as possible to break the automatic cycle of the habit you want to change.

Tend to your relationships

A common thread throughout the book is that you are the best person to know what is going on in your body and the only person who is in charge and can change things. That's not to say that you have to do everything on your own. Your relationships and social network can help you not only psychologically and practically, but also in boosting your immunity and health.

When you have a long-term condition, you will interact with more and more people. You may not like it. Still, the better you get at getting along with people, the easier it will get to manage your condition. Interacting with more people will not necessarily combat any feelings of loneliness and isolation that are not uncommon among people with long-term conditions. But it doesn't have to be this way. Having to manage a long-term condition can also give you more opportunities to get closer to family and friends and deepen your relationships.

When it comes to communicating with a health care professional or a family member, the key is to be clear about what you want to convey and express your opinions, feelings and questions. Also important is to avoid accusing others. Not only it is easy to misjudge their intentions and behaviours, but you are also not able to control what they think and do. You are responsible for expressing your own needs and getting what you want, not about changing other people's attitudes. Further, accusing people will make them more defensive and it is more likely for communication to break down.

It is essential to consider carefully the words you use when expressing your needs or feelings to not make them sound like judgements of the other person. Remember to start each statement with 'I', to signify that this is the way you feel about things and what you need.

Keep in mind that communication is a two-way process. While you may feel uncomfortable about expressing your feelings or asking for help, chances are that other people are also feeling the same way. It may be up to you to make sure the lines of communication are open. You cannot change the way other people communicate. What you can do is change your way of talking to make sure that you are understood.

Changing the way you speak is one aspect of improving your communication. Improving your listening is the other. Pay attention to the other person with compassion, feeling and insight. One basic principle is to seek to understand, before being understood.

An excellent technique to help you connect with the person you are talking to is called 'active listening' whereby you absorb what the other says without interrupting them. A technique to connect emotionally is to ask how the person feels about the situation or perhaps to make a statement about how you believe the person feels.

For example, your partner might say, "I've had enough, I'm doing everything around the house". An active listening response might be, "I can see this has upset you. Do you want to talk about it?" Whatever the answer, it is intended to clarify the facts or information being presented and to identify and respond to the emotions or feelings of the other person.

Letting go of your own opinions frees some mental energy to acknowledge the other person's views and emotions and helps you to help them. Giving people your full focus displays respect. When we feel respected, it is more likely we will remain calm and open for an honest conversation. And when you give someone such attention, you will gain more information from them. Not only by what they say, but you will also notice the tone of voice, body language and other clues to go beyond the words and gain insight into emotions.

When you are listening this intently to the other person show it. Think about your posture, lean in, retain good eye contact, nod and keep quiet. Giving a bit of white space when the other person has stopped talking gives them the chance to think about other things they want to add and allow you to think about your follow-up questions or comments.

Taking an active role in managing your condition is not easy, at least at first. Hopefully, the suggestions in this book inspired you. Still, even if you find this process difficult, the good news is that we get better at things the more we practise. Part of practising is monitoring our progress and tinkering with our plans. Over time, having a full and meaningful life while keeping on top of illness challenges will no longer seem so hard. Any change you can make and can stick with is better than nothing and will set off a virtuous cycle. When you identify activities close to your values, you will feel better. When you have an enjoyable day, it will help you sleep better. When you sleep better, you'll have fewer problems with your memory. Having fewer memory problems will make you less anxious. When you are less concerned, you'll have more energy to engage with the activities you enjoy.

Index

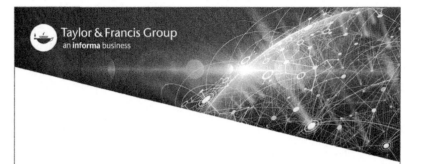